The Management of Pain in Older People:
a workbook

Pat Schofield

Barry Aveyard

Catherine Black

The Management of Pain in Older People
Pat Schofield, Barry Aveyard and Catherine Black
ISBN 978-1-905539-22-2

First published 2007

British Library Cataloguing in Publication Data
A catalogue record for this book is available from the British Library

Notice
Clinical practice and medical knowledge constantly evolve. Standard safety precautions must be followed, but, as knowledge is broadened by research, changes in practice, treatment and drug therapy may become necessary or appropriate. Readers must check the most current product information provided by the manufacturer of each drug to be administered and verify the dosages and correct administration, as well as contraindications. It is the responsibility of the practitioner, utilising the experience and knowledge of the patient, to determine dosages and the best treatment for each individual patient. Neither the publisher nor the authors assume any liability for any injury and/or damage to persons or property arising from this publication.

The Publisher
To contact M&K Publishing write to:
M&K Update Ltd · The Old Bakery · St. John's Street
Keswick · Cumbria CA12 5AS

Tel: 01768 773030 · Fax: 01768 781099
publishing@mkupdate.co.uk
www.mkupdate.co.uk

Designed & typeset in 11pt Usherwood Book by Mary Blood

Printed in England by Reed's Ltd. Penrith

The Management of Pain in Older People

Also available from M&K Publishing

All books can be ordered online at:
www.mkupdate.co.uk

Skills for Caring – A NEW series from M&K
Other titles in the series include

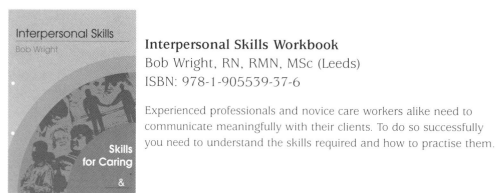

Interpersonal Skills Workbook
Bob Wright, RN, RMN, MSc (Leeds)
ISBN: 978-1-905539-37-6

Experienced professionals and novice care workers alike need to communicate meaningfully with their clients. To do so successfully you need to understand the skills required and how to practise them.

Loss & Grief
Bob Wright, SRN, RMN, MSc (Leeds)
ISBN: 978-1-905539-43-7

The feelings and thoughts connected with loss, grief, dying and death have always concerned people. The author is a specialist in crisis intervention. He has developed his experience in counselling and as a workshop facilitator over a number of years. This updated self-directed study workbook will appeal to everyone with a health and social care interest.

Coming soon
Nutritional Care of Older People Workbook
ISBN: 978-1-905539-05-3

Other M&K Publishing titles in print include

Routine Blood Results Explained
ISBN 978 -1-905539-38-3

Improving Patient Outcomes: a guide for ward managers
ISBN 978 -1-905539-06-1

Music Makes a Difference: A practical guide to developing music sessions with people with learning disabilities
ISBN 978 -1-905539-19-2

Contents

Tables

Figures

ABOUT THE AUTHORS

Pat Schofield RGN, PhD, PGDipEd, DipN

Pat has worked in the field of pain management since 1988. Initially as a specialist nurse and later as a lecturer and senior lecturer. She has been a member of the Council of the British Pain Society and is currently chair of their newly-formed Special Interest Group on Older People. Pat's research interests concern older people and she has carried out a number of research projects talking to residents living in care homes along with a systematic review of the literature on pain management in older adults and two annotated bibliographies on pain at the end of life and older adults. Pat has facilitated the pain management course for nurses for the past 19 years and has been responsible for developing part of the course as a distance learning programme.

Catherine Black MAEd, BA (Hons) Nursing, RN, RNT, Dip Health Services Manager

Catherine is a Senior Lecturer at the DHSS Education and Training Centre in the Isle of Man. Prior to this she was the Senior Sister at the St Bridget's Hospice in the Isle of Man. Catherine qualified as a nurse in 1990 and specialised in oncology, clinical trials and, more recently, palliative care. She worked at Weston Park Hospital in Sheffield and the University of Sheffield before returning to the Isle of Man in 2000. Her current interests include pain management, palliative care and research methodologies.

Barry Aveyard RMN, RGN, BA (Hons), CertEd, RNT, MA

Barry is qualified in both adult and mental health nursing. His experience covers a wide range of clinical settings; however working with older people is his key area of interest. He has worked in nurse education for several years as a teacher and lecturer and is also a member of the Royal College of Nursing Mental Health and Older People's Forum. He has published chapters and papers on various aspects of mental health in older people.

Introduction

This workbook is designed to give you a basic introduction to the management of pain in older people. It explores the size and nature of the problem, outlines some practical assessment and management approaches, and, finally, aims to help you think about the particular issues in your own area of practice.

The book is not designed to make you an expert in pain management but to increase your awareness of the complexity of the pain experience when you are working with older adults and to help you to understand the need for a creative and innovative approach to dealing with the person in your care who may be in pain.

At certain points, boxed areas are provided for you to write your own answers or reflections. (You could use your own notebook if you prefer.) At other points, you will be required to read around the subject and you will see this icon in the margin.

Opportunities for further study in a particular area are also included as "Further reading" sections at the end of individual chapters. For more resources on the management of pain in older people in general see "Appendix 3: Further reading and resources" at the end of the book.

1 Epidemiology of pain in the older adult

Pat Schofield

In *Pain and Suffering in the Elderly*, Harkins *et al.* (1990) begin with four important questions.

- What is the age-related epidemiology of pain problems?
- Is age a predisposing factor for chronic pain?
- Does the perception of pain decrease with age?
- Does age affect the diagnosis and treatment of pain in the clinical setting?

This workbook is intended to enable you to explore and answer these questions, while relating them to your own clinical practice.

AN AGEING POPULATION

> *'I'm tired – not just tired, but tired of being in pain.'*

The epidemiology of pain in the older adult has not been widely studied until recently. The International Association for the Study of Pain (IASP) has recently published some epidemiological information on their website for the Global Year against Pain in Older Adults (which is 2006–7). Some of this information will be discussed within this chapter. (For more information about this event see www.efic.org/week.html.)

The population is ageing worldwide and it is expected that there will be a rise in the over 65 age group by 17 per cent by 2050, meaning that over 65s will make up more than 36 per cent of the total population. The percentage over the age of 85 is expected to triple. Pain is very common amongst older people, with chronic pain affecting more than 50 per cent of older persons living in the community and, reportedly, more than 80 per cent of residents living in nursing homes (Ferrell, 1995; Helme & Gibson, 2001). Older people are more likely to be in pain than younger people.

Pain is the most frequently reported symptom by older adults, being reported by 73 per cent of older adults living in the community (Brody & Kleban, 1983) and it tends to be constant, of moderate to severe intensity and lasting for several years (Brattberg *et al.*, 1996).

Of those admitted into hospital, almost 46 per cent report pain, of which 19 per cent experience moderately or extremely severe pain and almost 13 per cent are dissatisfied with their pain control (Desbiens *et al.*, 1997).

Cancer is the second leading cause of death for adults over the age of 65 (D'Agostino *et al.*, 1990) and 67 per cent of cancer deaths occur in those over the age of 65 (Kennedy, 1995). Furthermore, Bernabei *et al.* (1998) highlighted in their study that 26 per cent of cancer patients over the age of 65 who are in daily pain did not receive any analgesia.

1

WHAT DO WE MEAN BY ELDERLY?

Before we can determine the incidence of pain in this population, we need to establish what we mean by 'elderly' people.

> The World Health Organisation (1993) has produced guidelines for the classification of older people. They suggest older people fall into three main categories. Identify these categories below.
>
> 1.
>
> 2.
>
> 3.
>
> Check your answers against the WHO classifications.
> http://whqlibdoc.who.int/hq/2001/WHO_NMH_NPH_01.2.pdf

However, the World Health Organisation (WHO) suggests that we should consider ageing to be a 'privilege' and a 'societal achievement'. It is also a challenge, which will impact on all aspects of 21st century society. (See the WHO website: www.who.int.)

There are many definitions of 'older people' and some flexibility is required; for example, the under 75 group may be dealt with by geriatricians but it is more likely that the over 75 age group will require specialist geriatric care as they are more likely to be frail. A third group is described as the oldest, sickest and most frail group with the most complicated medical problems (Hazzard *et al.*, 1994). But we must also remember that Nelson Mandela is one of our greatest world leaders and he is 88 years old!

> Consider the area where you work – what is the proportion of older people in each group?
>
> 1.
>
> 2.
>
> 3.

ALLEVIATING DISCOMFORT

There is no doubt that people are living longer today than ten years ago, although this does vary around the world. The World Health Organisation highlights that the very old (80 +) are the fastest-growing group. At the same time, there is a reduction in the birth rate and thus a reduction in the number of potential carers, supporters and people in work funding care through taxation.

Geriatric medicine is a highly-specialised area, as management of this group requires a very different perspective from that of younger generations. The spectrum of complaints, manifestations of distress and differential diagnosis are particular to older patients. For example, functional status is more important and recovery less dramatic.

Although many of the problems associated with ageing cannot be cured, much can be done to improve discomfort and disability which constitutes the 'art' of geriatric care (Ferrell, 1996).

THE AGEING PROCESS

Before we can consider issues surrounding pain in this group, we need to consider the theories of ageing and the normal bio-physiological processes that occur as the person becomes older. Gerontology is the study of ageing and geriatric medicine is classified as the medical care of the elderly.

 Read a section about physiology in a textbook on older people (several are listed in the references at the end of this chapter). What does it identify as the effects of ageing upon the major systems? Fill in the blanks below.

System	Effect of ageing
Skeletal system	
Skin	
Urinary	A 50% reduction in nephron units occurs. Blood flow to the kidney reduces therefore urine formation is reduced. Bladder problems occur as a result of muscle wasting.
Respiratory	
Cardiovascular	Degenerative heart and blood vessel disease. Fat deposits may form (atherosclerosis) and arteries may harden (arteriosclerosis). Hypertension is common in this age group.
Special senses	

These are important issues both for the pain experience and for the management of pain. The potential impact of pharmacological interventions for example, can be significantly influenced by the physiological system of the older person. This will be discussed later in Chapter 6.

THE PREVALENCE OF OLD AGE PAIN

As has been noted, the epidemiology of pain has not been well studied, but there are estimates which suggest that there are very high numbers of older people in pain.

> Think about the group that you work with. What type of painful conditions do they have?

Some of the conditions that you may have identified could be

- central post-stroke pain

- post-herpetic neuralgia

- arthritis

- cancer.

All of these conditions have been highlighted as being more prevalent in the older age group than in their younger counterparts. For example, osteoarthritis is common in 85 per cent of older people over the age of 65 and 60 per cent of cancers occur in the over 65 age group. Many of these conditions fall under the classification of **chronic pain** which is defined as:

> that which persists beyond the expected healing time, serves no useful purpose and may have no identifiable physical cause. (Merskey & Bogduk, 1992)

Chronic pain is defined in opposition to **acute pain** which is defined as:

> a sign of injury or disease, a warning that something is wrong causing the individual to seek help. (Merskey & Bogduk, 1992)

With any individual who has pain, the approach to management will be dependent upon the type of pain and whether it is acute or chronic. We will come back to this later.

 Read the article by Davis *et al.* (2002). Within this paper the authors identify the commonest causes of pain in older adults.

LACK OF RESEARCH

In spite of these findings, there has been surprisingly little attention globally to the issue of pain in older adults. For example, a review of 11 leading textbooks of geriatric medicine reveals only two chapters dedicated to the concept of pain and a review of eight geriatric nursing textbooks reveals less than 18 pages (out of 5000) dedicated to the management of pain (Ferrell, 1991).

This lack of research and education has allowed a whole range of beliefs and misconceptions to develop. For example, 'older people get used to pain' or 'pain is part of the ageing process'. These beliefs act as further barriers to effective pain management. We will refer to these again throughout the book.

When the older adult has dementia, the issue of pain becomes even more complex. Furthermore, because there are ethical issues around research in adults with dementia, the literature is particularly sparse. For example, some suggest that people with cognitive impairment tend to report less pain (Farrell *et al.*, 1996) and others, such as Parmalee *et al.* (1996), argue that evidence suggests that there is equal risk of pain in all older adults. This is further supported by Sengstaken and King (1993) who reported that, in their study, 66 per cent of people with cognitive impairment presented with chronic pain. More recent studies suggest that residents in care homes, where at least 75 per cent of the residents are cognitively impaired, do not tend to be taking oral medication for pain (Schofield & Payne, 2004, unpublished report).

Consider your patient group.

How many have cognitive impairment?

How many of those have an underlying potentially pain-producing problem?

SUMMARY

In this chapter, we have looked at the incidence of pain in the older population in the UK and the rest of the western world. Although there have been no major epidemiological studies, there is evidence to suggest that there is a problem and that it can be tackled by a number of actions related to the client group and the carers themselves.

References

Bernabei, R., Gambassi, G. and Lapane, K. (1998) Management of Pain in Elderly Patients with Cancer. SAGE study group. *Journal of the American Medical Association*, **279**, 1877–1882.

Brattberg, H., Parker, M.G. and Thorslund, M. (1996) The Prevalence of Pain Amongst the Oldest Old Living in Sweden. *Pain*, **67**, 29–34.

Brody, E.M. and Kleban, M.H. (1983) Day-to-day Mental and Physical Health Symptoms of Older People: A report on health logs. *Gerontology*, **23**, 75–85.

D'Agostino, N.S., Gray, G. and Scanlon, C. (1990) Cancer in the Older Adult: Understanding age related changes. *Journal of Gerontological Nursing*, **16**, 12–15.

Davis, G.C., Heimenz, M.L. and & White, T.L. (2002) Barriers to Managing Chronic Pain of Older Adults with Arthritis. *Journal of Nursing Scholarship*, **34**(2), 121–126.

Desbiens, N.A., Mueller-Rizner, N. and Conners, A.F. Jr (1997) Pain in the Oldest Old During Hospitalization and up to One Year Later. *Journal of the American Geriatric Society*, **45**, 1167–1172.

Farrell, M.J., Katz, B. and Helme, R.D. (1996) The Impact of Dementia on the Pain Experience. *Pain*, **67**, 7–15.

Ferrell, B.A. (1991) Pain Management in Elderly People. *Journal of American Geriatric Society*, **39**, 64–73.

Ferrell, B.A. (1995) Pain Evaluation and Management. In *Quality Care in Geriatric Settings*, ed. P.R. Katz, R.L. Lane and M.D. Mezey. New York: Springer.

Ferrell, B. (1996) Patient Education in Non-drug Interventions. In *Pain in the Elderly*, ed. B. Ferrell and B. Ferrell. Seattle: International Association for the Study of Pain Press.

Harkins, S.W., Kwentus, J. and Price, D.D. (1990) Pain and Suffering in the Elderly. In *The Management of Pain*, ed. J Bonica. Philadelphia: Lea and Febiger.

Hazzard, W.R., Bierman, E.L. and Blass, J.P. (1994) *Principles of Geriatric Medicine and Gerontology*. New York: McGraw Hill.

Helme, R.D. and Gibson, S.J. (2001) The Epidemiology of Pain in Older People. *Clinical Geriatric Medicine*, **17**, 417–431.

Kennedy, B.J. (1995) Age Related Clinical Trials of CALGB. *Cancer Control*, **2** (Suppl. 1), 14–16.

Merskey, H. and Bogduk, N. (1992) *Taxonomy of Pain Terms and Definitions*. Seattle: International Association for the Study of Pain.

Parmalee, P.A., Smith, B. and Katz, I.R. (1993) Pain Complaints and Cognitive Status Amongst Elderly Institution Residents. *Journal of the American Geriatrics Society*, **41**, 517–522.

Sengstaken, E.A. and King, S.A. (1993) The Problems of Pain and its Detection Among Geriatric Nursing Home Residents. *Journal of the American Geriatric Society*, **41**, 541–544.

Further reading

Gagliese, L. and Melzack, R. (1997) Chronic Pain in Elderly People. *Pain*, **70**, 3–14.

2 Physiological and biochemical changes

Pat Schofield

 To complete this chapter, it will be useful to read about some of the concepts underpinning the physiology of pain. See Davis (1993) and Melzack and Wall (1991).

HOW PAIN IS PROCESSED

A certain amount is known about what happens in the nervous system when a disease or injury arises and yet, even now, many questions are still unanswered and research into the mechanisms is ongoing. In this section, we will discuss the normal physiological concepts and then consider the issues that are particularly relevant for the care of older people.

THE NERVE FIBRES

If you put your hand onto a hot stove, you initiate a series of responses within the nervous system that will eventually be perceived as pain. The whole process begins at the site of the injury (where the hand touches the stove). There we have a group of nerve fibres that begin the process.

Complete the table below.

Nerve fibre	Myelin sheath	Type of sensation
a-delta		
c		Dull aching
a-beta	Yes	

You will have identified that the first group of nerve fibres to begin the process of transmission are a-delta nerve fibres which transmit the initial sharp shooting pain. They transmit extremely fast with the impulses reaching the brain at a rate of over 120 m per second. As they begin to transmit, they also start to release chemical substances which in turn activate the c fibres.

These chemical substances are known as **Substance P and prostaglandins**.

> Can you name the drug commonly taken for pain relief, which can reduce the effects of Substance P and prostaglandins?

We will come back to the third group of nerve fibres later.

7

> Although they register pain, the a-delta and c fibres are not known as pain fibres. Because they detect injury they are known by a name which comes from the Latin word for injury.
> Do you know what this is?

It is the a-delta and c fibres which transmit the sensation of pain into the nervous system. They respond to chemical, thermal and mechanical stimuli. It is important to be aware of this in order to understand the concepts of neuropathic and nociceptive pain.

Can you identify the differences between **neuropathic** and **nociceptive** pain?

Neuropathic pain is related to nerve injury whereas **nociceptive pain** is tissue damage and trauma related. This means that neuropathic pain is not opiate responsive but nociceptive pain is.

> Can you identify some neuropathic conditions that you have seen in practice? Two examples are given to start you off.
>
> Neuropathic pain
>
> Diabetic neuropathy

The common terms for these types of pain are acute and chronic. (See Chapter 1 for full definitions of acute pain and chronic pain from Merskey and Bogduk (1992).)

THE SPINAL CORD

The next stage of the pain processing pathway is the spinal cord. Both a-delta and c fibres enter the spinal cord at the dorsal horn. They then cross over to the opposite side of the spinal cord and begin to travel to the brain via the spinothalamic tract. Various structures in the brain are then involved in this process, for example the limbic system which activates fear and autonomic processes and the reticular activating system which depends upon sensory input. Pain provides a source of that sensory input.

At the dorsal horn we have a synapse and it is here that the body can prevent pain messages getting through by producing its own chemical substances which attach to receptors at this point. These chemicals are very similar to morphine.

Do you know what the body's own painkilling chemicals are called?

Consider a marathon runner. After running for about 10 to 15 miles, the runner experiences excruciating pain, but if they continue to run they pass through what is known as the 'pain barrier'. At this point the pain begins to subside because the person has started to produce the endogenous opioids which act like morphine and control the pain. While we are all capable of producing these chemicals, most of us tend to ask for drugs instead of relying upon our internal mechanisms to control the pain. It has been suggested that it can take a few days to get these opioids out of the system.

THE ROLE OF THE BRAIN

The impulses continue to pass to the brain along the spinothalamic tract, but there is no one centre in the brain that is responsible for pain processing. Therefore almost all of the brain becomes involved, making pain often difficult to treat.

Read about the role of the brain and then complete the table below, identifying the functions of some of the major structures of the brain.

Structure	Function
Cortices	
Thalamus	
Limbic system	Activates fear and autonomic processes
Reticular activating system	

The a-delta and c fibres exist throughout the body, on the periphery, viscera and internal organs with one exception. There is one place where we do not feel pain. (Think of Hannibal Lecter!) The internal substance of the brain has no pain receptors.

COPING WITH PAIN

A-BETA FIBRES

Back to the third group of nerve fibres, a-beta. These are much larger than the other two and therefore can transmit their sensations much more quickly, thus blocking the pain messages being carried by the other two. These fibres are activated by being rubbed.

Can you think of any pain relieving techniques that work on this principle? One example is given to start you off.

> Massage

We will come back to some of these approaches in later chapters.

THE PAIN GATE (THE GATE CONTROL THEORY OF PAIN)

The pain gate is situated in the spinal cord and was identified by Melzack and Wall back in 1965. They isolated a group of cells that could act like a gate to a farmer's field. If the gate is closed the pain messages cannot get through but if it is open they can and so we feel pain. These cells are called *substantia gelatinosa*.

Over the last 30 years, since the discovery of the pain gate the management of pain has changed dramatically, with a growing recognition of the contribution to pain management that can be made by members of the multi-disciplinary team.

Going back to the hand on the stove, the concept of the pain gate means that we have the mental ability to override the pain by 'descending inhibitory control' or positive thinking.

Can you think of any pain relieving techniques that we use that can close the gate in this way? One example is given to start you off.

> Relaxation

Accepted thinking on the pain gate has been updated in recent years. Read Dickenson (2002).

THE PAIN THRESHOLD

We all know that pain is individual. Therefore, two patients with the same condition may respond very differently. Patient A may be up and about while Patient B is lying in bed, not moving.

What are some of the factors that make pain an individual experience?

Age – do older or younger people cope better?

Gender – do males or females cope better?

Any other factors?

Now read Seers (1987).

Many factors are known to contribute to the individuality of pain or the pain threshold. This threshold is the amount of pain that an individual is prepared to tolerate and it can vary hour to hour, day to day and is influenced by a combination of the factors identified above. We also know that, as health professionals, we can influence this threshold by how we react to patients when they are in pain.

Here are some of the things that you probably identified as factors that make pain an individual experience.

Figure 2.1

Factors influencing the pain threshold

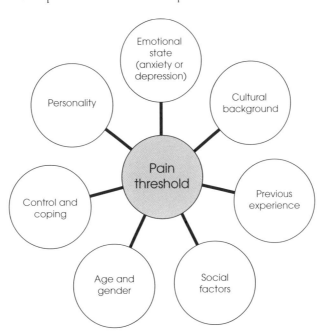

THE ROLE OF PRACTITIONERS

Consider the following statements – are they true or false?	
Nursing/medical staff attitudes have no effect upon the patient's pain	True/False
Giving information makes the pain worse	True/False
Listening to patients' fears, previous experience and coping strategies can reduce pain	True/False
Staff are in the best position to know what the patient is experiencing	True/False
All pain procedures have the same amount or level of pain	True/False
Self medication/patient-controlled analgesia makes the pain worse	True/False

Apart from the factors that are internal to the individual we are also influenced by those around us. For example, as carers it is important to consider how we respond to those in pain. What is the attitude of staff towards those in pain?

> Consider the place where you work. How do you and your colleagues respond to someone in pain? Are you empathetic or do you sometimes avoid the person, maybe because you do not know what to do or say?

Many years ago Jack Hayward published *Information: A prescription against pain* (1975). This study was repeated by Jennifer Boore in 1978 and published as *Information: A prescription for recovery* (1978). Both studies demonstrated that giving people information gave them control and, as a result, they were able to cope better. It has taken us many years to adopt these principles. But we are getting better at giving information.

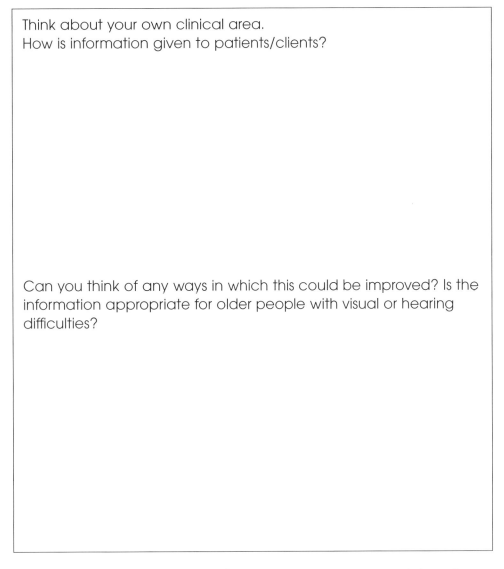

Think about your own clinical area.
How is information given to patients/clients?

Can you think of any ways in which this could be improved? Is the information appropriate for older people with visual or hearing difficulties?

It is often difficult to find time to listen to patients. Sometimes it is easier to resort to pharmacological approaches. But allowing someone to express their fears and worries is sometimes all that is needed to make them feel better.

Furthermore, people tend to employ their own ways of coping and this may be something totally different from what you would expect (such as acupuncture). Giving the person time to express their preferences may be very enlightening.

It is often said that you need to be a patient to know what it is like and this is also true of pain. We cannot see another person's pain and so we have to believe what they are telling us. As the philosopher Ludwig Wittgenstein (1967) wrote:

> I can only know that I am in pain – I have to accept what someone is telling me as I cannot see their pain.

How many times have you heard someone say 'they've only had their appendix removed, they should not be in that much pain' or 'they should be on oral analgesics by now'? These are example of pre-conceived expectations often held by nursing and medical staff which ultimately lead to poor pain control.

13

TYPES OF ANALGESIA

Finally, there is an issue about the control that is associated with type of analgesia. Whenever patients come into hospital, we take their medications from them and expect them to ask when they need it – which naturally makes the pain worse. Self-medication systems and patient-controlled analgesia can help prevent this.

To summarise, all of the factors highlighted in this chapter can influence the whole pain experience. Consider a patient in your care. How many of these factors are involved in their pain experience? The physiological and biochemical mechanisms and the factors influencing pain together form what is sometimes known as the 'puzzle of pain'.

DEFINING PAIN

Now that we have looked at the mechanisms of pain, it is useful to be able to define pain.

> Pain is what the experiencing person says it is and occurs when he/she says it does. (McCaffery 1968)

It has been suggested that this definition is a little simplistic. It also assumes that the individual has a command of language that we can understand. But what about those who are learning disabled or cognitively impaired or babies? They cannot tell us they have pain and so, traditionally, they have received little attention within the literature. A more appropriate definition is that proposed by the International Association for the Study of Pain (IASP):

> an unpleasant sensory or emotional experience associated with actual or potential tissue damage or described in terms of such damage. (Merskey & Bogduk, 1994)

We also have various categories of pain. We alluded to this earlier when we talked about the differences between nociceptive and neuropathic pain – and in Chapter 1 when we looked at the epidemiological issues of pain.

List below the types of pain condition seen in your area of practice, divided into acute and chronic pain.

Acute pain	Chronic pain

We must not forget cancer pain, as there are many patients experiencing pain as a result of cancer in many clinical settings. However, cancer pain can be acute or chronic and as such it should be treated according to whichever is the major category in any particular case. Furthermore, cancer pain is often dealt with by the specialist oncology or palliative care services and we address it as a specialist area in Chapter 8.

OLDER PEOPLE IN PARTICULAR

We have discussed the concepts underpinning pain processing. How does this relate to the older adult? Do older people have more or less pain than their younger counterparts?

In terms of physiological changes, there is little evidence to support the fact that anything happens to the pain pathways as we get older. Whilst patients can occasionally be admitted with silent myocardial infarctions and abdominal catastrophes in the older age group, there is no evidence to suggest that pain pathways deteriorate with age at all.

However, it is recognised that one of the problems associated with pain in older adults is co-morbidity – the presence of other conditions which may influence the perception of pain. These might include cognitive impairment, cardio-vascular disease or neuropathic disease (Weiner & Hanlon, 2001).

The prevalence of dementia doubles every five years from age 60. It rises from two per cent at age 60 to four per cent at age 70 and reaches 30 per cent at 85 years (Helme & Katz, 2003). Some also suggest that the prevalence of pain appears to decrease with increased cognitive impairment. However, there is no evidence to support the theory that pain processing changes with dementia and so we have to treat all people the same regardless of their age or cognitive ability.

Write down a situation from your practice where an older person with or without cognitive impairment was in pain.

1. How was this situation handled by the staff?

2. How did you know that this person was in pain?

continued overleaf

---

3. What have you learned from this?

4. How will you deal with the situation differently in the future based upon your new knowledge?

Many of us know when someone is experiencing pain and we need to be confident in our perception and deal with it. We talk about being the patient's advocate. Recognising pain and doing something about it is fundamental to the principles of advocacy. Principals of advocacy and pain are as follows:

- recognising pain-provoking situations
- pre-empting pain
- fostering a multi-disciplinary approach to pain management.

(Fordham, 1988)

SUMMARY

In this chapter we have looked at the physiology of pain: how pain is transmitted in the body, how we cope with it and how we attempt to define it. We have also looked at the particular challenges of managing pain in older people, such as co-morbidity and cognitive impairment.

References

Boore, J. (1978) *Information: A prescription for recovery*. London: Royal College of Nursing.

Davis, P. (1993) Opening Up the Gate Control Theory. *Nursing Standard*, **7**, 25–27.

Dickenson, A. (2002) Gate Control Theory of Pain Stands the Test of Time. *British Journal of Anaesthesia*, **88**(6),755–757.

Fordham, M. (1988) Pain. In *Patient Problems: A research base for nursing care*, ed. J. Wilson-Barnett and L. Batehup. London: Scutari Press.

Hayward, J. (1975) *Information: A prescription against pain*. London: Royal College of Nursing.

Helme, R.D. and Katz, B. (2003) Chronic Pain in the Elderly. In *Clinical Pain Management: Chronic pain*, ed. T. Jenson, B.Wilson and A. Rice. London: Arnold.

McCaffery, M. (1968) *Nursing Practice Theories Related to Cognition, Bodily Pain and Man-Environment Interactions*. Los Angeles: UCLA.

Melzack, R. and Wall, P. (1991) *The Challenge of Pain*. London: Penguin Books.

Seers, K. (1987) Perceptions of Pain. *Nursing Times*, **83**, 4837–4839.

Weiner, D. and Hanlon, J. (2001) Pain in Nursing Home Residents: Management strategies. *Drugs & Ageing*, **18**, 13–29.

Wittgenstein, L. (1967) *The Philosophical Investigations*. New York: Anchor Books.

3 The importance of communication

Barry Aveyard

The importance of using good communication skills in healthcare environments cannot be over-estimated. If we cannot communicate effectively with those we are caring for then we will never be able to meet their care needs fully. This is especially true when working with older people in the area of pain assessment and management. It is, however, important not to make assumptions about the kind of communication issues that we might face. In other words, not all older people are deaf, blind or confused.

Thorough and accurate assessment is vital if we are to achieve a meaningful person-centred approach to care. We should not make assumptions about a person's abilities or deficits. Where there are communication problems then assessment and control of pain might be more challenging. We will need to think carefully and clearly as to how we can best ensure that we meet that person's needs.

> In your own clinical experiences what communication difficulties have you experienced that might have made assessment of an older person's pain difficult?

17

DEMENTIA

Dementia is an umbrella term used to describe a number of different brain disorders that have in common a loss of brain function that is usually progressive and devastating in nature for the individual and those around them. There are potentially over a hundred different diseases that might be described as a type of dementia (Alzheimer's Society, 2003). The most common types are Alzheimer's Disease, vascular dementia and Dementia with Lewy Bodies. Common symptoms of dementia include memory impairment, confusion and problems with speech and understanding.

Alzheimer's Disease

Alzheimer's Disease is the most common form of dementia. It is characterised by the presence of an abnormal protein in the brain which causes damage to neurones and by impairment of the chemicals in the brain (neurotransmitters) which are associated with memory processing.

People with Alzheimer's Disease may experience difficulty with memory and struggle to name familiar objects and people. As the condition progresses they may:

- become more confused and struggle to remember recent events

- become increasingly withdrawn and experience loss of confidence

- experience regular periods of fear and anxiety as they struggle to make sense of their surroundings.

Vascular dementia

The most common type of vascular dementia is multi-infarct dementia which is caused by a series of small strokes, or 'mini-strokes', that often go unnoticed and cause damage to the cortex of the brain. It is important to be aware that some people who experience a significant vascular incident in the brain which causes a 'stroke' may also experience cognitive impairment along with their more observable physical symptoms.

Vascular dementia affects people in many different ways and the speed of the progression varies significantly from person to person. Whilst many of the symptoms of vascular dementia are very similar to those of Alzheimer's Disease, issues specific to vascular dementia might be:

- some physical weakness associated with stroke

- a 'stepped' progression, with symptoms remaining at a stable level and then suddenly deteriorating (this is a result of a further vascular change in the brain).

Dementia with Lewy Bodies

Dementia with Lewy Bodies (DLB) or Lewy Body Disease is characterised by small, spherical protein deposits found in nerve cells. Their presence in the brain damages neurones and impacts the brain's normal functioning. People who have DLB will usually have some of the symptoms of Alzheimer's and Parkinson's Diseases. As well as experiencing difficulties with memory and orientation, they will also experience muscle stiffness and slowness of movement and may shuffle when walking. Key elements of the condition are that people will often experience hallucinations and their cognitive ability can fluctuate even from hour to hour.

Person-centred care (Kitwood 1997) is often seen as an essential element of providing good quality dementia care. Basically this approach stresses the need always to see the person with dementia as a person with individual needs and not treat them as simply somebody-with-dementia. It is important to remember that each person will respond to their dementia in an individual way. There is no clear pattern of behaviour or progression of the disease. Everyone will need to be assessed as an individual. It is not useful to assume that any single assessment tool will meet the needs of every person.

The importance of education for nurses on the subject of pain assessment in dementia care has been clearly articulated by Scherder and van Manen (2004) in a study where they examined the assessment of pain in people with dementia.

What experience have you had of assessing pain in a person who has dementia?

 Visit the Alzheimer's Society website (www.alzheimers.org.uk) and read the fact sheets on the common types of dementia.

COMMUNICATING WITH A PERSON WITH DEMENTIA

Communicating with a person with dementia can be seen as a real problem. It is often assumed that a person who has lost the use of language skills is no longer able to communicate. The reality is that everything a person does is an attempt to communicate. Behaviour that is labeled as difficult and challenging may well be an attempt to communicate feelings of anger and frustration. This could make assessing pain in a person with dementia highly complex (Buffum *et al.*, 2001).

As has been made clear each person must be treated as an individual. However, the following general points may help promote better communication with a person who has dementia.

- Listen carefully to what the person has to say.
- Make sure that you have the person's full attention before you speak.
- Pay attention to body language.
- Speak clearly.
- Think about how things appear to the person with dementia.
- Consider whether any other factors are affecting their communication.
- Use physical contact to reassure.
- Show the person respect.

(Alzheimer's Society, 2005)

Whilst these things will help promote better communication there is still a challenge in ensuring that you are able to assess pain when a person has dementia. It is important to be aware of non-verbal pain indicators:

- moans or groans
- facial grimaces or winces
- clutching, either self or objects
- restlessness
- rubbing or massaging the affected area.

(Horgas, 2003)

What other non-verbal signs of pain can you identify?

It may not be appropriate to use the same pain assessment tools for all patients.

ACUTE CONFUSION

Acute confusional states most often result from an underlying physical illness and are considered to be temporary and reversible. They may be caused by diseases of body systems other than the brain, by poisons, by fluid/electrolyte or acid/base disturbances and by infections such as urinary tract infections or pneumonia. Factors that cause delirium are numerous and varied.

Because there is a danger that any older person who is confused may have dementia, there is a risk that other factors that might cause confusion are overlooked.

> Will pain exacerbate acute confusion? If so how might a person communicate this?

Rigney (2006) clearly highlights the challenge to nurses in being able to recognise acute confusion or delirium, suggesting that nurses must be able to distinguish delirium and its causes from other conditions such as dementia. If they are not able to do this, then the wellbeing of patients is at significant risk.

SENSORY PROBLEMS

It is clearly wrong to make assumptions that all older people are deaf or blind or have other sensory impairments. It is, however, important to be aware that we are all likely to experience some degree of sensory deficit as we age, and that this will have some impact upon how we are able to communicate at times.

How would you use a visual analogue scale to assess pain in a person who is not able to see clearly? How might you communicate as part of a pain assessment in a busy and noisy environment with a person who can not hear you clearly? Sensory deficit can be a serious barrier to effective communication with older people and so must be taken into consideration in pain assessment and management.

Practitioners should be prepared to consider different and innovative techniques. Harper and Bell (2006) advocate the use of multi-dimensional approaches to pain assessment where patients have communication difficulties. They suggest that a pain assessment tool should be able to reflect patients' perception of their pain.

> What factors need to be taken into account for optimal pain assessment in a person with sensory deficit?

Summary

In this chapter we have looked at the obstacles to communication that can occur when working with elderly patients to manage their pain. Dementia of various kinds has been identified, as well as confusion and sensory impairment. However, there are many techniques to facilitate understanding in these circumstances which will be covered in subsequent chapters.

References

Alzheimer's Society (2003) *What is Dementia?* Information sheet. London: Alzheimer's Society.

Alzheimer's Society (2005) *Communication.* Information sheet. London: Alzheimer's Society.

Buffum, M.D., Miaskowski, C. and Sands, S. (2001) A Pilot Study of the Relationship between Discomfort and Agitation in Patients with Dementia. *Geriatric Nursing,* **22**(2), 80–85.

Harper, K. and Bell, S. (2006) A Pain Assessment Tool for Patients with Limited Communication Ability. *Nursing Standard,* **20**(51), 40–44.

Horgas, A.L. (2003) *Assessing Pain in Persons with Dementia: Best practices in nursing care for hospitalized older adults with dementia.* New York: The John A. Hartford Institution.

Kitwood, T. (1997) *Dementia Reconsidered.* Buckingham: Open University Press.

Rigney, T. (2006) Delirium in the Hospitalised Elder and Recommendations for Practice. *Geriatric Nursing,* **27**(3), 151–157.

Scherder, E. and van Manen, F. (2004) Pain in Alzheimer's Disease: Nursing assistants' and patients' evaluations. *Journal of Advanced Nursing,* **52**(2), 151–158.

4 Assessment of pain

Barry Aveyard and Pat Schofield

In this chapter we will identify and discuss issues surrounding pain assessment and the approaches to assessment that are available to us in everyday practice. We will then consider some of the particular problems that may be encountered when dealing with an older person and, finally, identify some pain assessment tools that have been developed specifically for this group.

In September 1990, the Royal College of Surgeons and the Royal College of Anaesthetists published a report of their working party on pain after surgery. This report can be accessed from your local library or anaesthetic department. It makes recommendations regarding the management of post-operative pain in the UK. Since that time, many of the recommendations have been taken on board for all aspects of pain.

One of the key recommendations was that pain assessment should be recorded by nursing staff alongside other routine observations of blood pressure and pulse. It is now generally accepted that pain should be recorded in this way and pain charts are incorporated into observation charts in many areas.

WHY RECORD PAIN?

Now read Schofield (1995) and Schofield & Dunham (2002).

Benefits of carrying out a formal assessment of pain

- Improved understanding
  By using an assessment we are able to determine which approaches are effective and this will help us to be more creative and innovative in our approach to pain management.

- Formal records
  By presenting a formal evidence-based record of our assessment of pain we are more likely to convince other members of the team of the need for intervention and we are able to highlight when strategies are not working.

- Faster recovery
  By assessing pain we are more likely to treat it more effectively which will, in turn, improve care and subsequent recovery.

- Patient reassurance
  If we are talking to patients in an open, honest way about their pain then they will feel more relaxed and in control, which will help them to cope better.

- Legal requirement
  Legal judgments have been passed where pain assessment has not been documented within the medical or nursing notes and compensation has been paid to relatives regarding ineffective pain control. If assessment has not been carried out, then pain management may well be ineffective. As highlighted previously, the Royal College of Surgeons and the Royal College of Anaesthetists suggest that pain assessment is the start of the process of pain management.

- Professional accountability
  It is a Nursing and Midwifery Council requirement that all registered nurses maintain their records and any documentation errors can result in disciplinary hearings.

RECORDING PAIN APPROPRIATELY

Before we can begin our pain assessment the following factors may be important:

- the environment in which the assessment is taking place;

- and whether the pain is acute, chronic or cancer pain.

The approach to assessment will need to be adapted to our clinical situation. It would clearly be unrealistic to spend hours completing lengthy pain assessment charts in a really busy accident and emergency department where the priority of care is saving lives.

Furthermore, the type of patient is an important consideration. A person in highly acute pain will not want to answer a whole range of questions about their pain; they will want you to take action to relieve the pain as quickly as possible. However, the person with chronic pain may want to discuss their pain at length and so this assessment will be more complex and detailed. The patient with cancer may easily become tired and need a different style of assessment again. We need to be aware of a range of pain tools and be able to adapt them to suit differing situations and our particular patient or client group.

Which pain assessment tool is used in your area at the moment?

List the advantages and disadvantages

Advantages	Disadvantages

We will return to this later.

FACTORS TO RECORD

Before any pain assessment can be carried out, there are certain factors that need to be considered:

- quality
- onset
- pattern
- treatment
- effects
- intensity
- understanding
- goals.

Table 4.1
Assessment of pain

Rationale	Question
Quality	Can you describe your pain. Is it burning, shooting, stabbing?
Onset	When did the pain start. How did it start?
Pattern	Does it come and go? Is it better at certain times?
Treatment	What are you using at the moment to manage your pain?
Effects	What makes it better/worse?
Intensity	How severe is it?
Understanding	What do you think is causing your pain?
Goals	What do you want us to do for you?

These are important questions that must be addressed. But if the pain is severe and acute it must be assessed and managed quickly and efficiently. The most important issue is intensity as this is the aspect that we will come back to when we evaluate treatment.

EVALUATING INTENSITY

There are several measures of intensity:

- Visual Analogue Scale
- Numerical Rating Scale
- Verbal Descriptors
- Faces Pain Scale
- Colour Scale.

These all have individual strengths and weaknesses and may have different applications when being used with older people.

VISUAL ANALOGUE SCALE

This is a 10 cm line with 'no pain' at one end and 'worst pain imaginable' at the other end. The patient is asked to rate the level of pain that they are currently experiencing. The end point descriptors should not be changed.

Figure 4.1
Visual Analogue
Scale

No _____ Worst pain
pain   imaginable

This scale can be completed by children as young as five, all the way through the age spectrum to older adults, although some older adults may struggle with the concept. This is a simple tool that has wide application. It is easily understood if it is explained clearly.

NUMERICAL RATING SCALE

This is a visual analogue scale with numbered ratings along the line. These can be 0 to 10 or 0 to 5.

Figure 4.2
Numerical rating
scale

0_____1_____2_____3_____4_____5_____6_____7_____8_____9_____10

This is similar to the Visual Analogue Scale in terms of application. It is also simple to use and easily understood. However, there may be a temptation to choose a particular number rather than the actual position on the scale that represents the pain experience.

VERBAL DESCRIPTORS

This is a number of boxes that are labeled 'none', 'mild', 'moderate' and 'severe' and can be ticked by the patient or member of staff.

Figure 4.3
Verbal Descriptors

☐ Severe

☐ Moderate

☐ Mild

☐ None

The limited range of options offered by this tool may be restrictive in the descriptions of pain. Occasionally people say that their pain is worse than mild but not really severe. More boxes could be added but this may invalidate the tool or confuse the respondent.

FACES PAIN SCALE

The Faces Pain Scale was first introduced for children, as it was found that they could relate to the expressions on the faces in terms of how they were feeling (Wong & Baker, 1988).

It has since been found that some adults prefer this tool! But do not be tempted to use it with older adults as they can perceive this as offensive and pertaining to mood as opposed to pain.

Figure 4.4
Faces Pain Scale

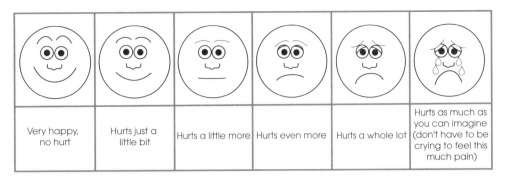

Very happy, no hurt	Hurts just a little bit	Hurts a little more	Hurts even more	Hurts a whole lot	Hurts as much as you can imagine (don't have to be crying to feel this much pain)

Adapted with permission from Whaley, L. and Wong, D. Nursing Care of Infants and Children, 3rd edn, p. 1070. ©1987 by C.V. Mosby Company.

COLOUR SCALE

This is also based upon the Visual Analogue Scale and uses colour to indicate increasing severity of the pain. Thus red is associated with very severe pain and green/blue represents none to mild pain. However, this may be confusing for some people who cannot relate to the concept of colour.

McGILL PAIN QUESTIONNAIRE (MPQ)

A final and important pain measure is known as the McGill Pain Questionnaire (MPQ). Developed by Melzack and Torgerson (1975), it was designed to measure the quality of pain. The investigators carried out research to identify the various words that people use to describe their pain. They then tested these descriptors and refined them to form the tool. The questionnaire now contains 78 descriptors and has been translated into 18 languages.

It is seen as the most reliable and valid measure of pain quality and often used in the field of chronic pain. It has been used in children as young as five and through to older adults. Although it only takes five minutes to complete and five minutes to analyse, many practitioners find it too complicated for everyday use. However, it is useful for patients who are unable to describe their pain, as it can help them to put it into words.

Think of a time when you last experienced pain. What words would you use to describe it? (Not easy, is it?)

27

Now read Melzack (1975). Look at the scale – are any of your descriptors on the list?

Go back to the pain assessment tool used in your area. How do you think it compares to the tools outlined above?

Are you happy that your tool is evidence-based?

Has it been adapted?

Would you consider using a more appropriate tool?

Can you identify groups of patients who would not be able to complete any of the scales?

Many groups have communication problems which may require different pain assessment tools:

- babies
- people with learning disabilities
- people with cultural differences
- older people
- unconscious patients.

The Visual Analogue Scale has been translated into several languages for non-English speakers (see www.britishpainsociety.org). There is also a large body of literature that highlights assessment tools for people in intensive care units or high dependency units. We will focus on assessment tools for older adults.

PAIN ASSESSMENT IN THE OLDER ADULT

A recent review of the literature related to pain assessment highlighted 42 papers written since 1995 that use various different pain assessment tools with the older adult (Schofield et al., 2005). There has clearly been very little research related to this group and more work is needed. In general, it has been demonstrated that this age group prefers the Verbal Descriptors (none, mild, moderate, severe) or the Numerical Rating Scale. The research supports the belief that the Faces Pain Scale is inappropriate and is generally misunderstood to be an indicator of mood.

> What do you think are the main problems with assessment of pain in the older adults encountered within your area of practice?

There is a danger in making assumptions about older people when thinking about pain assessment. Older people are all unique and individual; it is not helpful to assume that there can be one pain assessment measure that can be universally used with older people. However some factors that might be worthy of consideration are:

- cognitive impairment
- communication difficulties
- motor loss
- sensory impairment.

(Bird, 2005)

It has been suggested that nurses and other healthcare workers should pay particular attention to listening to older people when assessing their pain (Evans 2004). The person may want to take their time to explain how the pain is affecting them and the impact it is having upon their life, especially when the person is experiencing chronic pain. It may be that their story provides key information about pain intensity that may not be captured by the use of a single pain measure.

It also important to think about the level of skills required in order to carry out a good quality pain assessment. Harper and Bell (2006) highlight the importance of education and training for nurses in the field of pain assessment, especially when working with patients who have communication difficulties.

When working with older adults, there is the additional problem of a high incidence of dementia. As already discussed, the incidence of dementia increases dramatically with increasing age. If you are working with the oldest population, the chances are that there is dementia present and, consequently, undiagnosed pain.

Look at your patient group.

How many have dementia?

How many have potential pain-producing conditions?

How many are taking analgesics?

Are those with dementia taking different forms of analgesia to those without?

Those with dementia are less likely to be taking analgesics.

PAIN BEHAVIOURS

As Sternbach (1974) has observed:
  In order to describe pain it is necessary for the patient to do something ...
  in order for us to determine that he is experiencing pain.

Early research identified several major behaviours that were indicative of pain:

- verbal complaints
- para-verbal sounds (sighs, moans)
- body posture/gestures (limping, rubbing, guarding)
- functional limitations.

Later studies reinforced this research and identified behaviours that could be rated and measured:

- verbal complaints
- downtime
- standing posture
- body language
- stationary movement
- non-verbal/vocal
- grimaces
- mobility
- equipment use
- medication use.

(Keefe & Block, 1982)

These indicators are generally referred to as 'intuitive' indicators. As mentioned earlier, there have been a number of pain assessment tools developed based upon these behaviours.

Take a look at Abbey *et al.* (2004) and Wary *et al.* (2004). Both papers demonstrate pain assessment scales that have been specifically designed to meet the needs of the older adult with cognitive impairment.

How many behavioural indicators are encompassed within these scales?

Think of your own practice. Can you identify any patients whose care would be enhanced by using a behavioural pain scale? Try it out and see whether you can effectively identify pain using the scale.

Summary

In this chapter, we have looked at why we record pain and what factors need to be recorded for effective pain management. We have surveyed the various assessment tools available and identified the Numerical Rating Scale and Verbal Descriptors as the most popular tools for older adults. We have also established that there are a number of scales specifically designed for use with older adults with cognitive impairment. You should now be able to make a plan for implementing pain assessment in your own clinical area.

References

Abbey, J., Piller, N. and DeBellis, A. (2004) The Abbey Pain Scale: A 1-minute numerical indicator for people with end-stage dementia. *International Journal of Palliative Nursing*, **10**(1), 6–13.

Bird, J. (2005). Assessing Pain in Older People. *Nursing Standard*, **19**(19), 45–52.

Evans, C. (2004). Improving Assessment of Pain in Older People. *Emergency Nurse*, **12**(5), 18–21.

Harper, K. and Bell, S. (2006). A Pain Assessment Tool for Patients with Limited Communication Ability. *Nursing Standard*, **20**(51), 40–41.

Keefe, F.J. and Block, A.R. (1982). Methods for Assessing Low Back Pain. *Behaviour Therapy*, **13**, 363–375.

Melzack, R. and Torgerson, W.S. (1975). The McGill Pain Questionnaire: Major properties and scoring methods. *Pain*, **1**, 277–299.

Schofield, P.A. (1995). The Assessment of Pain and Analysis of Tools. *Professional Nurse*, **10**(11), 703–706.

Schofield, P.A. and Dunham, M. (2002). Pain Assessment: How far have we come in listening to our patients? *Professional Nurse*, **18**(5), 276–279.

Schofield, P.A., Clarke, A., Dunham, M., Faulkner, M., Howarth, A. and Ryan, T. (2005) Assessment of Pain in Adults with Cognitive Impairment: A review of the tools. *International Journal on Disability and Human Development*, **4**(2), 59–66.

Sternbach, R.A. (1974). *Pain Patients: Traits and treatments*. New York: Academic Press.

Wary, B., Filbet, M. and Villard, J.F. (2004). *Using Doloplus with Non-verbal Cognitively Impaired Elderly Patients*. Available at http://www.doloplus.com.

Waley, L. and Wong, D. (1987). *Nursing Care of Infants and Children*. 3rd edn. London: Mosby.

Wong, D. and Baker, C. (1988). Pain in Children: Comparison of assessment scales. *Pediatric Nursing* **14**(1), 9–17.

5 The role of the multidisciplinary team

Pat Schofield

Many years ago when pain clinics were first introduced, they tended to consist of single specialists with an interest in pain management. These early clinics offered invasive treatments based upon the medical model of 'cure'. Since the introduction of the Gate Control Theory of Pain in 1965, the development of multidisciplinary pain management has evolved dramatically around the world. Furthermore, there is increasing evidence to support the effectiveness of a multidisciplinary approach (Dysvik *et al.*, 2004; Guzman *et al.*, 2002), although limited research has been carried out with older adults. This chapter will identify the contributions that can be made by the individual members of the multidisciplinary team and enable the reader to consider their own areas of practice and ways in which multidisciplinary team collaboration may be enhanced or developed to improve the management of pain.

 You may find it useful to refer to the following resources as you work through this chapter: Pringle (1993); Poulton & West (1993); the Department of Health website – www.dh.gov.uk; the Royal College of Anaesthetists website – www.rcoa.ac.uk.

THE TEAM MEMBERS AND THEIR ROLES

It has long been recognised that the multidisciplinary team is essential to provide pain management according to the bio-psychosocial model of care needed to deal with the problems associated with chronic conditions. Pharmacological and invasive interventions alone are not enough to deal with the more complex psychosocial aspects present with chronic illness.

A multidisciplinary team needs:

● healthcare professionals who are dedicated to the patient group

● clearly-defined roles and responsibilities

● clearly-defined aims and objectives

● strong lines of communication at all levels.

Can you identify the members of the multidisciplinary team working in your area. What are their roles?

Team member	Role
e.g. Nurse	*Caregiver, advocate, liaison*

continue over page if necessary

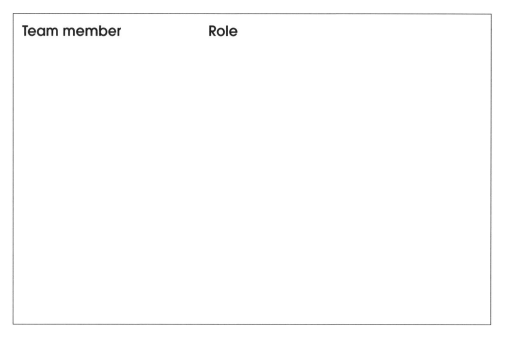

Team member	Role

The multidisciplinary team working in pain management should have a clear mission statement with aims and objectives that are focused on the adoption of pharmacological, non-pharmacological and cognitive behavioural coping strategies.

According to the Royal College of Anaesthetists and the British Pain Society (2003) the objectives of a chronic pain service should include:

- alleviation of pain

- alleviation of psychological and behavioural dysfunction and distress

- reduction of disability

- rationalisation of medication

- reduction of utilisation of healthcare services including consultations in primary and secondary care, surgical operations and treatments such as physiotherapy

- attention to social, family and occupational issues

- education for nursing, medical staff and other allied healthcare professions

- continuing audit and evaluation of the service and the needs of patients

- outcome measures for patients with chronic pain

- research into epidemiology, causes and management of chronic pain.

(The Royal College of Anaesthetists & The British Pain Society, 2003)

They further recommend that the ideal staffing regime should consist of the following personnel:

- medical practitioners

- non-consultant career grade doctors

- nurse specialists and nurse consultants

- clinical psychologists

- physiotherapists.

34

Interdisciplinary contact may be required with the following healthcare professionals:

- general practitioners
- rehabilitation medicine specialists
- occupational health specialists
- psychiatrists, including specialists in addiction medicine
- palliative care physicians
- other hospital specialists
- occupational therapists
- pharmacists
- vocational counsellors.

Talk to or visit your local pain clinic, if you have one, and find out which members of the multidisciplinary team work here. Find out about their roles.

Specialist	**Role**
Consultant	
Nurse specialist/Nurse consultant	
Psychologist	
Physiotherapist	

PAIN MANAGEMENT PROGRAMMES

One major development in the field of pain management has been the introduction of pain management programmes. Following the introduction of the Gate Control Theory (1965), practitioners began to manage chronic pain using the bio-psychosocial model which attempts to modify the individuals' thoughts and beliefs about their pain. This led to the introduction of multidisciplinary pain management programmes.

The goals of pain management programmes are as follows:

- to improve the patient's understanding of their situation
- to improve the patient's level of physical functioning despite ongoing pain

- to reduce the patient's perceived level of pain and suffering

- to provide coping skills and strategies for dealing with chronic pain, disability, distress and life changes

- to promote self-management to reduce the patient's future reliance on others, such as for medication management and therapy

- to reduce or modify the patient's future use of healthcare services

- to return the patient to their pre-pain state with regard to activities of daily living.

It is appropriate to consider a multidisciplinary pain management programme for the individual when:

- there has been a failure of medical and surgical treatment

- there is a perception of over-reliance on medications and therapies

- there is pronounced inactivity

- there is significant depression or anxiety

- there is a perception of inadequate coping

- the individual is receptive to adopting a self-management approach and is willing to participate in such a programme.

It should be recognised that not all patients are suitable for a group-based pain management programme and individual therapy may be required.

Multidisciplinary pain management programmes have an increasing evidence base to support their use in reducing suffering and pain perception. The success of these programmes is in the adoption of a cognitive behavioural approach to management. Techniques taught should reinforce:

- pain coping strategies – to prevent patients from relying on passive and ineffective strategies such as catastrophising (panicking), which are likely to cause high levels of pain and psychological distress resulting in maladaptive pain behaviour.

- self-efficacy beliefs – assisting the patient to believe in their personal ability to manage their pain and emotional distress.

- anxiety management strategies – assisting the patient to reduce avoidance behaviours in response to fear of painful exacerbation or re-injury.

Multidisciplinary pain management programmes generally contain four components:

- identifying and challenging specific maladaptive attitudes, beliefs, thoughts and expectations

- modifying unhelpful behaviour

- managing emotional distress – including doubt, guilt, anger, anxiety, depression, loss, poor self-esteem and fear of the future – more effectively

- understanding and applying quota-based or time-contingent activity-enhancement.

They might involve a graduated activity programme, an education programme and a lifestyle modification programme, examples of which are outlined below.

Graduated activity programme

- Reduce inactivity and avoid physical deconditioning.

- Increase daily activity (despite pain) to improve overall physical functioning.

- Address fear-avoidance behaviour by introducing education relating to 'hurt and harm', teach pacing and goal setting as well as the introduction of a graded 'desensitisation' programme to allay specific fears.

Education programme

This would involve teaching the patient:

- concepts and constructs with regard to the varieties of pain, the underlying physical changes with chronic pain and the differences between 'hurt' and 'harm'

- concepts of illness and disability – from medical, psychological and social perspectives – as well as patient opportunities and responsibilities

- the scientific basis of pain and pain pathways including the Gate Control Theory

- about analgesic and co-analgesic drugs, their risks, benefits and likely effects

- effective physical activity and manual handling with regard to activities of daily living and potential vocational rehabilitation.

Lifestyle modification programme

- goal setting

- pacing techniques

- daily planning

- ways to access community involvement

- communication skills

- appropriate ergonomics for all daily activities

- return-to-work skills

An appropriate programme would take advantage of the dynamics of a group setting over a period of time (typically varying between two weeks full time and six weeks part time). There should be sufficient intensity to suit the complexity of the enrolled patients and the use of a range of health professionals to deliver a consistent and repeated theme.

Pain management programmes have the capacity to improve the patient's quality of life, reduce suffering and distress and provide a more satisfying daily lifestyle. They are not designed to eliminate pain or provide the patient with a cure.

THE MULTIDISCIPLINARY TEAM AND OLDER PEOPLE

In the past, outcome studies for pain management using multidisciplinary treatment programmes were few and far between. It was suggested that older adults were more difficult to treat and often resistant to psychological therapies. They adopted a more passive method in dealing with disease and, because of the risk of cognitive and physical impairments, they were less likely to be considered suitable for complex treatment programmes.

However, a review of the pain treatment studies has shown that 10 out of 13 studies reported some benefit from multidisciplinary treatment (Gibson *et al.*, 1996).

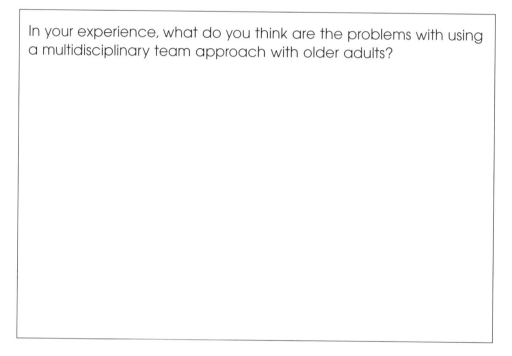

In your experience, what do you think are the problems with using a multidisciplinary team approach with older adults?

A recent doctoral thesis evaluated the effectiveness of cognitive behavioural therapy (CBT) with attention support within a group of nursing home residents in Canada (Cook, 1995). From a potential pool of 104 residents, 28 were recruited and assigned to two groups. The programme was conducted over a period of ten weeks and included teaching the residents a range of skills including education, re-conceptualisation, relaxation, imagery, diversion and cognitive restructuring. The results of the study support the findings of others who demonstrate positive effects of psychologically-based interventions and the author suggested that CBT can be applied to nursing home residents.

However, he did suggest that there would need to be recognition of the needs of residents, flexibility would be required and that the approach can be time-consuming for staff. But, CBT has the potential to reduce medication intake and nursing care in pain management of this group. Kerns *et al.* (2001) also report a case study of a 72-year-old man referred to a pain centre and offered the opportunity to take part in CBT. This study further supported the work of Cook and concurs with the premise that CBT is appropriate for older adults. Another study, by Strine (2002), was carried out to evaluate nursing home residents randomly assigned into a biofeedback or waiting list control group. The participants were monitored for ten weeks and the study demonstrated that biofeedback is another possible approach that could be adopted for nursing home residents to reduce pain. As with all of the studies discussed so far, the main problem is related to small sample sizes and Strine did not discuss levels of cognitive impairment, which raises the issue of the level of cognitive ability required in the older adult for them to be usefully included in such a programme. Nevertheless, viewed collectively, the above studies do support such approaches in this group and are certainly worth further study.

Recently, a study by Schofield involved talking to residents living in care homes about their pain and identified four major themes:

- a reluctance to report pain and an acceptance that pain is normal with low expectations of help from medical interventions

- fear of chemical or pharmacological interventions

- differences in age-related perceptions of pain

- lack of awareness of potential pain-relieving strategies.

(Schofield, 2006)

Within this chapter we have considered the multidisciplinary approach to pain management, pain management programmes and how this approach may be beneficial in managing the various aspects of pain experienced by the older adult.

Consider some of the other staff listed below. Talk to them and see whether they can offer alternative approaches for the older adults in your care.

Pharmacist

Occupational therapist

Carer

Dietician

Speech therapist

Summary

In this chapter we have seen that it is evident that older adults have a fear of traditional methods of pain management. Evidence to support the multidisciplinary team approach to their care is lacking but where studies exist they do appear to demonstrate that older adults can respond well to cognitive behavioural approaches. It would seem reasonable to assume that multidisciplinary team management is an effective approach for any individual with chronic pain, regardless of their age.

References

Cook, A. (1995) *Cognitive behavioural pain management for elderly nursing home residents.* Doctoral thesis, University of Manitoba.

Dysvik, E., Guttormsen, V.A. and Eikeland, O. (2004) The Effectiveness of a Multidisciplinary Pain Management Programme Managing Chronic Pain. *International Journal of Nursing Practice*, **10**, 224–234.

Gibson, S., Farrell, M., Katz, B. and Helme, R. (1996) Multidisciplinary Management of Chronic Non-malignant Pain in Older Adults. In *Pain in the Elderly*, ed. B. Ferrell and B. Ferrell. Seattle: IASP Press.

Guzman, J., Esmail, R., Karjalainen, K., Malmivaara, A., Irvin, E. and Bombardier, C. (2002) Multidisciplinary Bio-psychosocial Rehabilitation for Chronic Low Back Pain. *Cochrane Library*, **2**. Chichester: Wiley.

Kerns, R., Otis, J.D. and Marcus, K.S. (2001) Cognitive Behavioural Therapy for Chronic Pain in the Elderly. *Clinics in Geriatric Medicine*, **17**(3), 503–523.

Pringle, M. (1993) *Change and Teamwork in Primary Care.* London: BMJ Publishing.

Poulton, B.C. and West, M.A. (1993) Effective Multidisciplinary Teamwork on Primary Health Care. *Journal of Advanced Nursing*, **18**, 918–925.

Royal College of Anaesthetists & The Pain Society (2003) *Pain Management Services: Good practice.* London: Royal College of Anaesthetists.

Schofield, P.A. (2006) Talking to Older People in Care Homes: What are their perceptions of pain and preferred pain management strategies? A pilot study. *British Journal of Nursing*, **15**(9), 509–514.

Strine, G.N. (2002) *Self reports of pain reduction through paced respiration and heart rate variability biofeedback with nursing home residents.* Doctoral thesis, Widener University.

Further reading

Association of Anaesthetists (1997) *Provision of Pain Services.* London: The Association of Anaesthetists of Great Britain and Ireland & The British Pain Society.

6 Pharmacological management of pain

Pat Schofield

This chapter introduces the issues involved in prescribing medications for older adults. Whilst nurses often do not prescribe, it is important for them to understand the nature of pharmacological interventions for pain management and to be aware of the potential contraindications and complications that can exist as a result of pre-existing co-morbidities.

 It may be useful for you to read 'Medicines and older people, implementing medicine-related aspects of the NSF for older people' on the Department of Health website (www.dh.gov.uk).

Other useful websites would be:

- Department of Health website – www.dh.gov.uk
- Bandolier website – www.jr2.ox.ac.uk/bandolier
- International Association for the Study of Pain website – www.iasp-pain.org
- British Pain Society website – www.britishpainsociety.org
- Pan American Health Organisation website (in particular for the three-step analgesic ladder) – www.paho.org.

Pharmacological management is often one of the first steps taken in the management of many pain problems. However, there are several issues that we do need to take on board when dealing with older adults in particular:

- whether the pain is neuropathic or nociceptive
- pre-existing co-morbidities which may affect metabolism
- current medication and potential contraindications/side effects
- the potential for non-pharmacological interventions in conjunction with pharmacological interventions
- issues of concordance.

As long as these issues have been identified there is no reason why pharmacological interventions cannot be successfully used with the older adult.

 It may be useful to read Drago (2007).

Identify the commonly-used medications in your practice area.

41

THREE-STEP ANALGESIC LADDER

In 1989, the World Health Organisation (WHO) introduced the 'three step analgesic ladder'. This has been widely used as a guide for the management of cancer pain and it is now recognised as a useful guide for all types of pain.

Recently, the ladder has been reviewed and judged still appropriate today (see PAHO website – www.paho.org).

Figure 6.1

The three-step analgesic ladder

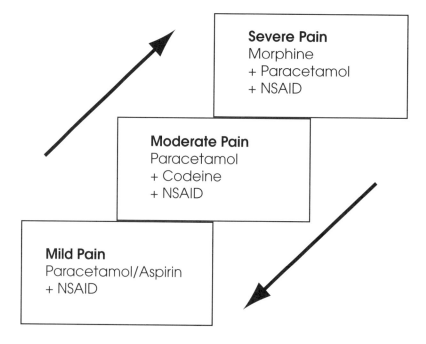

Severe Pain
Morphine
+ Paracetamol
+ NSAID

Moderate Pain
Paracetamol
+ Codeine
+ NSAID

Mild Pain
Paracetamol/Aspirin
+ NSAID

MILD PAIN

Paracetamol

Paracetamol is readily available over the counter and in many over-the-counter preparations such as cold and 'flu remedies. It is the preferred analgesic for older adults with musculo-skeletal problems and can be used for some mild forms of neuropathic pain. In terms of dosing, no reduction is necessary for older adults, although care should be taken not to exceed the 4 g maximum limit in 24 hours (8 x 500 mg). Liver damage may be more likely when there is fasting, dehydration, poor nutrition and high alcohol consumption.

While aspirin is recognised on step 1 as being a good analgesic drug with anti-inflammatory effects, the potential side effects tend to mean that it is avoided in practice.

MODERATE PAIN

Codeine

Codeine is often used for acute, predictable incident pain and can be used alone or in one of many formulations combined with aspirin or paracetamol. Some individuals have a congenital absence of enzyme required to transform codeine into morphine (methylmorphine) which means that pain relief is not achieved. codeine can cause constipation, confusion and nausea and the conversion process can be inhibited by some common medications (cimetidine, haloperidol, Amitriptylline and many SSRIs (Fluozxetine)).

List some of the commonly-used co-analgesic formulations used in practice.

Some co-analgesic drugs contain less than the therapeutic dose of codeine.

Table 6.1

Combination analgesics available on NHS prescription

Generic name	Constituents	Available without prescription?
co-codamol	codeine 8 mg paracetamol 500 mg	Yes
co-codaprin	codeine 8 mg aspirin 400 mg	Yes
co-dydramol	dihydrocodeine 10 mg paracetamol 500 mg	No
co-proxamol	d-propoxyphene 32.5 mg paracetamol 325 mg	No
aspav	papaveretum 10 mg aspirin 500 mg	No
colpadol/tylex/kapake	codeine 30 mg paracetamol 500 mg	No

Tramadol

Tramadol is a weak, centrally-acting analgesic with some action upon opioid receptors. Tramadol has significant additional pharmacological actions including the inhibition of noradrenaline and serotonin re-uptake, so it is classed separately from traditional opioids. Approximately one-third of patients cannot tolerate Tramadol and experience symptoms such as nausea, vomiting, sweating, dizziness, tremors and headaches. Serious side effects include delirium and hallucinations.

SEVERE PAIN

Opioid therapy

Well-established for the treatment of cancer pain, opioids are being increasingly used for the treatment of chronic pain (see The British Pain Society – www.britishpainsociety.org).

> List some of the commonly-used opioids from your area of practice

Morphine is considered the gold standard. It is derived from the opium poppy and it is from morphine that many of the other opioids are derived, diamorphine (or heroin) being one such derivative that is commonly used in practice. (Diamorphine does have links with drug abuse and so is not available in some parts of the world.)

Recently, there have been a number of synthetic opioids developed that are less prone to have centrally-acting effects and so are less likely to cause problems with addiction.

Table 6.2
Opioid drugs

Drug	Routes	Dose range	Duration
morphine	po/im/iv/sc	5 mg	3–4 hrs
diamorphine	po/im/iv/sc	2.5 mg	3–4 hrs
fentanyl	iv/topical/ea	50–200 ug	10–20 mins
methadone	po/im/sc	5–30 mg	6–8 hrs
papavertum	im/iv/sc	10–20 mg	3–4 hrs
pethidine	po/im/iv	25–150 mg	2–3 hrs
buprenorphine	sl/im/iv	0.2–2 mg	6–10 hrs

im: intra-muscular iv: intra-venous sc: subcutaneous sl: sublingual po: oral

Many healthcare professionals have concerns that patients will become addicted to opioids – this is known as opiophobia (Morgan, 1986). To clarify, let us look at the recognised definitions of addiction, tolerance and dependency.

Addiction

A behaviour of overwhelming involvement with obtaining and using drugs for psychic effects

Tolerance

A (physical, psychological, pharmacological) need for ever-increasing doses of a drug

Dependency

A state which leads to withdrawal symptoms when a drug is abruptly stopped.

44

It is clear that tolerance and dependence do not necessarily imply addiction. Yet we often see evidence of opiophobia in practice where staff delay, withhold, under-administer or under-prescribe opioids.

The general rule for prescribing opioids with older adults is to 'start low and go slow'. Nevertheless, there are a number of side effects associated with opioid use that should be anticipated and dealt with, to prevent patients from stopping taking them. For example, constipation and nausea are common and should be prevented by using anti-emetics and a good bowel regime with a faecal softener where necessary. Drowsiness is common in the first few days of prescription and so patients should be warned that this will occur and is quite normal.

Several opioids should be avoided with older adults or used with caution. For example pethidine should be avoided as its metabolite – norpethidine – can cause excitement, agitation, twitching and tremors. Fentanyl patches are not appropriate for patients who have not taken opioids previously. Methadone accumulation is more common in older adults, which results in an increase in half-life from six hours to up to two to three days.

Non-Steroidal Anti-Inflammatory Drugs (NSAIDs)

Non-Steroidal Anti-Inflammatory Drugs (NSAIDs) are analgesics comparable to paracetamol, but paracetamol is preferred, particularly in the older adult. These drugs have many side effects, particularly for the older person and should therefore be used with caution (Sinatra, 2002).

NSAIDs with short half-lives – such as ibuprofen and diclofenac – appear to have fewer side effects. Both selective and non-selective COX-2 inhibitors cause water and sodium retention, increased blood pressure and peripheral oedema and reduced glomerular filtration rate. Therefore caution should be used when prescribing in older adults with cardiac failure, hypertension or renal impairment.

Adjuvant analgesics

Neuropathic pain is now commonly treated with anticonvulsant and antiepileptic drugs:

- burning pain – anticonvulsant drugs

- shooting pain – antiepileptic drugs.

Drugs such as Amitriptylline are used independently of the antidepressant effect and provide pain relief more rapidly than the mood-elevating effect at a much lower dose. For example, the dose for depression is up to 150 mg while the dose for pain is around 10 mg, increasing slowly every three to seven days to between 30 and 50 mg. Side effects of the tricyclic antidepressants include dry mouth, postural hypotension, falls, constipation, sedation and urinary retention.

Anticonvulsant drugs are used for neuropathic pain:

- for trigeminal neuralgia – carbemazapine

- for diabetic neuropathy and post herpetic neuralgia – gabapentin

- for neuropathic pain – sodium valproate.

Older adults will need pre-treatment counselling for some of these preparations as they can omit some of the tablets if they become confused as to their use in pain control and think that they are for depression.

Topical agents

Analgesic gels and creams can be prescribed or bought over the counter and they have been found to be helpful as an adjuvant. NSAID creams can be more beneficial than purely topical creams such as lidnocaine as they have anti-inflammatory properties also. Capsasin (hot chilli peppers) has some evidence of efficacy for diabetic neuropathy and post-herpetic neuralgia. However, some older adults may be reluctant to use it because of the burning effect of the cream.

Older people do undergo distinct changes in their physiology due entirely to age and not to pathological processes. On the other hand, all drugs have the potential to be poisonous regardless of the age of the individual. We must remember that pain should always be treated using a multimodal approach.

Age-related changes apply specifically to body composition. Water, muscle and fat volumes change naturally with age, as do the cardio-vascular system, the hepatic and renal system and the integumentary system. These changes slow reflexes, reduce muscle strength and alter the delicate homeostatic mechanism which maintains the internal environment of the body at optimal levels. In health, these changes do not pose a major problem to the individual. However, in disease and ill health which requires pharmacological interventions, these changes do need to be incorporated into the management equation, especially in terms of dose and time interval. Such changes include:

- musculo-skeletal changes
- cardiovascular changes
- hepatic changes
- renal changes
- sensitivity changes.

OTHER CONSIDERATIONS

Apart from the obvious factors associated with pharmacology, including side effects, contraindications and dosing, there are a number of age-related specific factors that should be taken into account.

Older adults, like any other age group will respond better to treatment if they are given the opportunity to make an informed choice. Therefore, explanation is essential, giving the person the opportunity to ask questions and to decide whether or not they wish to participate in the treatment plan.

Drugs should be labelled clearly and the rationale and timings clearly explained. It goes without saying that bottles should be accessible. Guidance regarding side effects and contraindications should be given so that the person does not experience any unexpected side effects. The aim of management should be discussed with the patient so that they are aware whether the treatment is aiming for pain control or reduction. Finally, doses should be as low as possible whilst providing a therapeutic effect and the whole regime must be closely monitored.

Consideration of all of these factors should encourage concordance and communication.

Summary

The selection of pharmacological treatments for older adults is often based upon limited evidence, particularly when dealing with the oldest old, who may be living in care homes. In this chapter, we have established that dosage should take into account the efficacy for the condition being treated, age-related metabolism, existing co-morbidities and potential side effects. Analgesic drugs are used to treat symptoms rather than cure. Attention to communication and information-giving, irrespective of the age of the patient, is paramount if concordance is to be achieved.

References

Drago, R. (2007) Management of Pain by Pharmacological Intervention in the Older Adult. In *The Management of Pain in Older Adults*, ed. P.A. Schofield. Chichester: Wiley.

Morgan, P. (1986) American Opiophobia: Customary under-utilisation of opioid analgesics. *Advances in Alcohol and Substance Abuse*, **5**(1–2), 163–173.

Sinatra, R. (2002) Role of COX-2 Inhibitors in the Evolution of Acute Pain Management. *Journal of Pain and Symptom Management*, **24** (Suppl. 1), S18–27.

Further reading

World Health Organisation (1994) *Pain Relief*. Geneva: WHO.

7 Snoezelen or 'sensory environments'

Pat Schofield

This chapter looks at the senses and the potential for providing a sensory environment or Snoezelen to aid relaxation for pain management.

 Schofield (2002) and Schofield & Payne (2002) may be of interest. You will also find information on Snoezelen at either of these two websites or you could visit your local facility.
World Snoezelen Foundation website – www.worldwidesnoezelen.com
ROMPA website – www.rompa.com

THE SENSES

Before we look at the concept of Snoezelen we need first to think about the senses.

Can you name the six senses?

1.   2.

3.   4.

5.   6.

You will have probably found the first five easy to name – taste, touch, sound, smell and sight. But did you identify the sixth sense? It is the kinesthetic sense – the sense of where we are in time and space.

We often take our sensory input for granted. Take a few minutes to appreciate the amount and types of sensory input you are currently experiencing. It is amazing but we usually only value our senses fully when we lose one of them – such as hearing or sight. Helen Keller was described as being more alive than many people and yet she could neither hear nor see.

Think about how powerful the senses are.

Vision – the sight of a beautiful view that we consider breathtaking or the changing colours of the trees as we move into spring or autumn.

Taste – the tastes of food that you enjoyed as a child.

Touch – a caring touch that has the power to make someone feel better.

Smell – the scent that can conjure up many memories.

Sound – the emotion aroused by a piece of music.

Kinesthetic – the sense of the position of our bodies and limbs, for example, sitting on a chair.

Throughout our lives we accumulate these sensory experiences and form a catalogue of memories which we can recall at any time or relive involuntarily when we experience the same sensory input. We tend to surround ourselves with pleasurable sensory experiences within our homes in order to help us feel safe, secure, calm and relaxed. But as we get older we can lose one or more of our senses.

Think about how this happens with age. Then complete the chart below.

Sense	Effect of ageing
Vision	
Hearing	
Smell	
Touch	
Taste	
Kinesthetic	

These are the effects of ageing on the senses that you have probably identified.

Vision – a slowing or reduction of visual processing speed, adaptation to dark/light, visual acuity. This can be caused by cataracts, diabetic neuropathy, CVA, glaucoma, vitamin deficiency, anxiety and arthritis.

Hearing – a loss of ability to tune out background noise, loss of high frequency. This can be caused by wax, infections, tinnitus, anxiety and hysteria.

Smell – a loss of acuteness, reduction in sensitivity. This can be caused by head injuries, inflammation, colds, nerve damage and smoking.

Touch – a general wear and tear, loss of heat control, decreased tactile sensitivity, heightened cold sensation. This can be caused by nerve damage, neuropathy, immobility and arthritis.

Taste – a dryness of mouth, 50 per cent reduction in the number of taste buds. This can be caused by nerve damage, olfactory sense and facial nerve damage.

Kinesthetic – diminished reflexes, slower voluntary movement. This can be caused by Parkinson's Disease, vertigo, drugs and anxiety.

Sensory restriction does occur as we get older, but it can also occur in other situations, for example being in hospital rooms that do not have windows or being in an unchanging environment for a long period of time.

This concept links to the Gate Control Theory. In Chapter 2 we talked about the role of the reticular activating system and how it depends upon sensory input to keep it busy.

If we, therefore, provide sensory input in the form of sensory stimulation or Snoezelen we can actually focus the attention of the brain away from the pain. This is part of the concept that underpins the use of Snoezelen for the management of chronic pain as discussed in Schofield (2002).

SNOEZELEN OR 'SENSORY ENVIRONMENT'

Snoezelen or sensory environment is a concept first highlighted by two workers at the DeHaartenburg institute for learning disabilities (Hulsegge & Verheul, 1987) in the Netherlands. The word 'Snoezelen' is said to be a contraction of two Dutch words meaning sniff and doze. The original concept was developed using simple effects, such as using coloured paper, light bulbs and tin foil to stimulate all of the primary senses simultaneously. However, Hulsegge & Verheul (1987) were reluctant to evaluate the concept in a formal way. It was two years later, in the UK, when the first empirical studies began to appear (Cunningham *et al.*, 1989).

Studies then highlighted the positive behavioural changes which occurred in a learning disabled group of adults (aged 19 to 70 years), with evidence of less self-injurious behaviour and an overall 'calming effect' (Haggar & Hutchinson, 1992). Since the original study in Chesterfield, the original Snoezelen centre there has developed and expanded into the first large-scale purpose-built facility at Ash Green Hospital, Chesterfield. It comprises a range of different rooms containing various lights, music, colours and textures all designed to stimulate the primary senses simultaneously. It can be used as both a distraction and relaxation type of environment.

RELAXATION

Being relaxed is considered to be extremely beneficial. Relaxation is a technique used by athletes, executives and patients in hospital. Being relaxed is defined as being in 'a state of consciousness characterised by feelings of peace and release from tension anxiety and fear' (Ryman, 1996).

Relaxation is a quietening and calming of the mind and a state of relative freedom from anxiety and muscle tension.

Based upon this definition, the following systems all experience a reduction:

- oxygen consumption
- respiratory rate
- heart rate
- muscle tension
- blood pressure
- alpha waves.

Physiologically, the relaxation response is the opposite of the fight-and-flight response and so we would expect to see a reduction in all of the systems identified above.

You can read about the relaxation response further in Benson *et al*. (1974).

What do you think are the advantages /disadvantages of using relaxation?	
Advantages	Disadvantages

Relaxation may not relieve pain but it does have many other benefits for people with pain as it does reduce muscle tension and anxiety, both of which exacerbate pain.

51

Some of the advantages which you should have identified include that it:

- aids sleep
- strengthens the nurse–patient relationship
- improves problem solving
- minimises stress
- reduces muscle tension
- increases self-control
- decreases fatigue
- distracts from pain
- enhances other pain relief measures.

Disadvantages include that it:

- suggests that pain is 'in the mind'
- is not a substitute for good pain management
- is not good for severe pain
- can cause side effects
- has time and resource implications.

 Read the article by Carroll & Seers (1998) for a good overview of the literature associated with relaxation and pain.

DISTRACTION

It could be suggested that it would be common sense to view distraction from the pain as a successful strategy for dealing with it. This approach involves focusing a patient's mind on something pleasant, away from the pain.

This is an approach often used by individuals with chronic pain when they do things such as reading or watching television. Also, it can be used with children, who can be distracted by bubbles, pictures and stories. This could be taken a step further in a Snoezelen environment and we will come back to this later.

For now, consider the advantages and disadvantages of using distraction with your patients.

Advantages	Disadvantages

Can you think of different ways of providing distraction for older people in hospital? It might help if you think about the type of things that you would do to distract yourself.

There are many forms of distraction, the simplest being just spending time to talk to a patient. As far back as 1963, Butler highlighted the significance of enabling older people to talk about their lives and recalling pleasurable memories. He termed this 'life review'. Another strategy that is commonly used in care homes is the introduction of pets which can provide a useful distraction for people who are used to having pets of their own. Alternatively, there is a great deal of interest in the use of music as part of a number of environmental factors that nurses may be able to influence (Biley, 1992).

Environmental factors

Read and consider Good (1995).

Think about the type of environment in which you work. Identify the nature of the environment using the table below as a guide. For example, what type of lighting do you have in your area? Are the lights switched off at night? Can patients see out of the windows?

Factor	Effect
Light	
Noise	
Colour	
Comfort	
Aromas	

There are a number of publications that discuss the potentially detrimental effects of environmental factors such as noise and colour (Biley, 1993; McGonigal, 1986; Topf, 2000) and there is considerable interest in promoting more positive environments.

53

What sort of things do you like to do to relax?

Sadly, the cold clinical settings in which we care for many of our patients are not conducive to relaxation.

As we have discussed earlier, anxiety and pain exacerbate each other. Anxiety causes muscle tension which in turn leads to pain. Someone who has pain will become anxious and this in turn will exacerbate their pain.

A reduction in anxiety can reduce pain and the best way to enable this is to allow the patient time to relax. A Snoezelen environment provides such an opportunity.

THE SNOEZELEN ENVIRONMENT AND RELAXATION

The Snoezelen environment is about enabling people to feel safe and secure and relaxed by providing pleasant sensory experiences. For example, there are bubble tubes, fibre optic sprays and oil slides that project changing colours upon an otherwise dull, colourless background. Soothing rhythmic music is piped into the room or even through a mattress to give a massage effect. Aromatherapy diffusers provide pleasant aromas and soft furnishings provide comfortable areas; there may even be a heated waterbed, ball pool or Jacuzzi for different tactile stimulation. Together these sensory experiences provide a distraction or an opportunity for relaxation that has been investigated in both pain and palliative care settings and has been shown to reduce both pain and anxiety.

The ultimate aim of the facility is to provide sensory stimulation to all of the primary senses simultaneously. If you consider the sort of environments that aim to promote relaxation, such as restaurants, they tend to use soft lighting, music, comfortable chairs, pleasant smells and, naturally, delicious tastes. This is a far cry from the traditional hospital environment. Even Florence Nightingale recognised the importance of the environment when she used to place her patients' beds outside when the sun was shining.

Think about how you would set up a Snoezelen room in your own clinical area. Some of the issues that you will need to consider are:

- cost
- resources
- equipment
- space
- access.

Summary

In this chapter, we have looked at the use of Snoezelen rooms or sensory environments in pain management. It may well be that you cannot afford the £1.5 million that it cost to set up the facility at Ash Green Hospital in Chesterfield and space is always at a premium. But there are many practices, hospitals and clinics that have managed to set up rooms despite cost and space restrictions. Your local Trust may have some information. Alternatively, you will find a lot of useful information on the two websites mentioned at the beginning of this chapter.

References

Benson, H., Beary, J.F. and Carol, M.P. (1974) The Relaxation Response. *Psychiatry*, **37**, 37–46.

Biley, F. (1992) Use of Music in Therapeutic Care. *British Journal of Nursing*, **1**, 178–180.

Biley, F. (1993) Ward Design: Creating a healing patient-environment. *Nursing Standard*, **8**(5), 31–35.

Carroll, D. and Seers, K. (1998) Relaxation for the Relief of Chronic Pain: A systematic review. *Journal of Advanced Nursing*, **27**(3), 476–487.

Cunningham, C.C., Hutchinson, R. and Kewin, J. (1989) Recreation for People with Profound and Severe Learning Difficulties: The Whittington Hall Snoezelen Project. In *The Whittington Hall Snoezelen Project: A report from inception to the end of the first 12 months*, ed. R. Hutchinson. Chesterfield: Chesterfield & North Derbyshire Health Authority.

Good, M. (1995) A Comparison of the Effects of Jaw Relaxation and Music on Post-operative Pain, *Nursing Research*, **44**, 52–57.

Haggar, L. and Hutchinson, R. (1992) Snoezelen: An approach to the provision of a leisure resource for people with profound handicaps. *Mental Handicap*, **18**, 51–55

Hulsegge, J. and Verheul, A. (1987) *Snoezelen: Another world*. Chesterfield: ROMPA International.

McGonigal, K.S. (1986) The Importance of Sleep and the Sensory Environment to Critically Ill Patients. *Intensive Care Nursing*, **2**, 73–83.

Ryman, L. (1995) Relaxation and Visualisation. In *The Nurses' Book of Complementary Therapies*, ed. D. Rankin-Box. Edinburgh: Churchill Livingstone.

Schofield, P.A. (2002) Snoezelen: An alternative environment for relaxation in the management of chronic pain. *British Journal of Nursing*, **11**(12), 811–819.

Schofield, P.A. and Payne, S.A. (2002) The Use of Snoezelen within Palliative Care. *International Journal of Palliative Nursing*, **9**(3), 124–130.

Topf, M. (2000) Hospital Noise Pollution: An environmental stress model to guide research and clinical interventions. *Journal of Advanced Nursing*, **31**(3), 520–528.

8 Cancer pain management in the older person

Catherine Black

Cancer is a disease that becomes more prevalent with age (Cooley & Coventry, 2003), and pain is one of the most common symptoms of cancer (Portenoy, 1992), occurring in more than 70 per cent of cancer patients (Mercadante *et al.*, 2006; Glare *et al.*, 2004). It follows that the particular issues associated with cancer pain in the older person are worth specific study.

This chapter will begin with a brief review of the causes of pain in the cancer patient. It will then examine the management of such pain from the pharmacological perspective with a particular focus on morphine, as this is the standard against which other analgesics for severe pain are measured (Hanks *et al.*, 2001). There are non-pharmacological ways of managing cancer pain but it is not in the scope of this chapter to address them. Once the information in this chapter is combined with an in-depth patient assessment, you should be able to enhance your skills when managing cancer pain in older people.

PHYSIOLOGY OF CANCER PAIN

Think of one or two individuals you have cared for who have cancer and who had pain. Identify the causes of that pain.

Cancer pain can be caused by a large number of factors. Cherny (2003) identifies over a hundred physical causes of pain for the patient with cancer. These can be grouped into the four categories (Ward 2000) outlined below, each of which can lead to pain that is acute or chronic.

PAIN CAUSED DIRECTLY BY THE TUMOUR

Tumour invasion causes the majority of ongoing pain for people with cancer (Fukshansky *et al.*, 2005). This pain is caused by direct tumour pressure or tumour invasion of surrounding tissue and so the type and location of such pain will be different for each person. Tumours can invade bone, nerves, viscera, blood vessels or mucous membranes leading to a vast diversity of problems such as ulceration and raised intracranial pressure. In each of these cases, the pain caused will be different not only in location but also in intensity and type of pain being described by the patient during assessment.

PAIN CAUSED BY CANCER INVESTIGATIONS OR TREATMENTS

Investigations (for example, lumbar punctures, biopsies and mammograms), surgery, chemotherapy and radiotherapy can all cause pain during the immediate treatment phase, and such pains tend to be acute. Chemotherapy can cause pain during intravenous infusion as well as ongoing problems due to the toxicity of the drugs, such as mucositis and peripheral neuropathy. Other treatments, such as bisphosphonates and hormones, can also cause pain as a side effect of the treatment. Surgery and radiotherapy can also lead to permanent tissue damage which may lead to chronic pain. In the case of radiotherapy, this may occur up to 30 years following treatment.

PAIN RELATED TO CANCER

Tumours can create obstructions of adjacent tissues, such as the lymphatic system, creating problems such as lymphoedema and ascites which can often produce pain. Cancer-related weakness and reduced mobility can also lead to painful problems such as constipation, pressure ulcers, and deep venous thrombosis.

PAIN UNRELATED TO CANCER

More than half of all cancers occur in people over the age of 65 years. Within this age group there is an increased possibility that the individual may also have concurrent patho-physiologies that can also cause pain, such as cardiac problems and degenerative changes to joints.

In 1989, Cicely Saunders identified that pain in the cancer patient has many causes and not all are physical. She called this concept 'total pain' and it is a key concept within cancer and palliative care. The concept of total pain suggests that any individual's pain experience has several components:

- physical pain

- psychological pain

- spiritual or existential pain

- social pain.

57

Figure 8.1
The components of
total pain

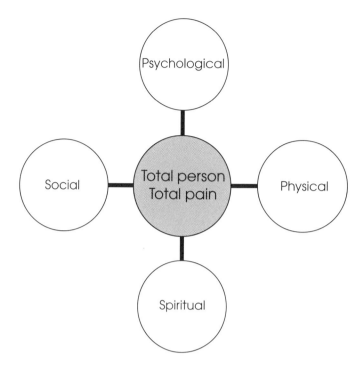

It is the combination of these factors that makes each pain experience unique.

For the cancer patient, an awareness of an increase in their pain may lead to a concern that this is an indication that the tumour is spreading, or that there have been problems with their treatment. An awareness of the impact of other factors on the pain experience allows us to recognise that, even though a patient's disease may not have progressed physiologically, their experience of pain may have increased as other factors have become increasingly important. Being diagnosed with cancer may affect their relationships with family and friends – for better and for worse – and this will impact the social aspect of their pain. They may also have questions about life and death which can lead to spiritual or existential pain.

For a more detailed discussion of the total pain read Greenstreet (2001) or Otis-Green *et al.* (2002), or visit www.symptomcontrol.com.

Review the cases you identified earlier. Can you now identify other causes of their pain which are not physiological?

ASSESSMENT OF PAIN

This key area was covered in Chapter 4. It is important to assess pain regularly and to use a standardised assessment tool that will ensure that all members of the healthcare team are making assessments in the same way so that valid comparisons can be made. It is also vital that, when assessing the pain of a person with cancer, the tool used allows for an assessment of all the aspects of total pain (Ward, 2000).

There is a view that older people with cancer have less pain than younger people. It may be that this group have less sensitivity to pain due to an age-related decline in nerve function, however it may also be that older people report pain less effectively (Portenoy, 1992). Mercadante *et al.* (2006) discuss how older people are more likely to report inadequate pain management than younger people.

Portenoy (1992) also raises the issue that, even if physiological pain perception is less in older people, there is a suggestion that they have fewer psychological and social coping strategies to deal with their pain, and so their experience of 'total pain' may be increased. Maxwell (2000) also highlights that unresolved pain reduces hope and increases depression. Rehabilitation then suffers with a subsequent decline in physical condition and an increase in falls. Appropriate assessment is a vital tool in the inequitable pain management related to ageing and helps to identify the factors that influence the total pain experience.

Reflect on what you learned in Chapter 4 and the information you have learned about the patho-physiology of cancer pain and total pain.
List the information that you would require to complete an accurate assessment of pain in a person with cancer.

The information required may include factors such as:

- location of pain
- causes of pain – particular movements, particular positions
- pain score – best, worst, average, current
- effectiveness of treatment or interventions in the last 24 hours
- which treatments or interventions had which effect
- how the pain makes the person feel
- how the pain limits the person's daily functioning
- how the pain makes the person's carers feel
- what the patient wants from pain relief.

In order to undertake a holistic assessment which reflects all aspects of total pain, the healthcare practitioner will be required to examine various aspects of the person's pain experience, some of which may not be captured by the pain intensity scales. The use of assessment tools is important but it must be supported by a further qualitative assessment where other issues concerning the meaning of pain to the person are explored.

This information may not necessarily be collected by the nurse or the doctor, and other members of the multidisciplinary team (such as the chaplain) can obtain important details. Careful documentation and consistent multidisciplinary ongoing evaluation and re-assessment are vital to the effectiveness of treatments.

MANAGEMENT OF CANCER PAIN

Once you grasp the concept of total pain, it becomes clear that the use of analgesia alone may not be enough to manage pain caused by cancer. However, the use of analgesia, and especially opioids, is one that causes practitioners most concern and so will be the main focus here.

List the treatments (drugs and others) you have experience of using to manage cancer pain. For each intervention, identify whether or not it is successful in your experience.

Treatment	Successful	Unsuccessful

Review the unsuccessful treatments and try to identify why they may not have achieved the results you hoped for.

PHARMACOLOGICAL TREATMENTS

The WHO three-step analgesic ladder provides the underpinning principles that should be used for managing cancer pain more than 75 per cent of cancer pain can be managed in this way.

Read either of the following for more information: Palliative Medicine (2004) or www.who.int/cancer/palliative/painladder/en.

Review the WHO three-step analgesic ladder and ensure that you are familiar with the classes of drugs listed. Make a list of the drugs that are commonly used in your area and the appropriate doses and routes of administration.

Review your list. Have you been using the drugs within their appropriate dose, route and frequency? Highlight any that you have not been using appropriately.

The analgesic ladder is only useful if it is used correctly and those prescribing the drugs and those administering the drugs make full use of them. There is still a concern that analgesia (opiates in particular) are under-prescribed and that they are subsequently administered in doses at the lower range of those prescribed.

Opiates

In 2004, a shortage of the supply of diamorphine for injection was highlighted by the Department of Health. This shortage is ongoing at the time of writing and so the focus will be on the use of morphine as the gold standard.

The starting dose for an opioid naïve patient of any age is 2.5 to 5 mg of morphine orally four hourly and should be given as needed. The strong opioids do not have a maximum dose but can be given as needed until the patient gets the level of pain relief they want while having manageable side effects. A study by Mercadante et al. (2006) found that elderly patients already receiving opioids are no more susceptible to side effects during such dose titration than younger adults, although older patients may require lower doses overall.

If the dose is not effective it can be repeated until an appropriate dose is found. At the end of each 24-hour period the total morphine taken should be calculated and divided by six to find the new four-hourly dose (Example 1).

Example 1	
Amount in 24 hours:	15 mg 4 hourly + 2 x 15 mg breakthrough doses = 90 mg + 30 mg = 120 mg in 24 hours
New daily dose required:	120 mg divided by 6 = 20 mg = 20 mg 4 hourly + 20 mg for breakthrough

This process may take several days, but once the patient is stable on a regular 4 hourly dose of morphine they can be converted to a long-acting dose that requires them to take less medication. This maybe preferable for people who have problems remembering to take their medication or have problems physically taking the drugs. The calculation for the conversion involves totaling the daily dose of morphine and dividing it into one or two doses depending on the form of controlled-release morphine to be used (Example 2).

Example 2		
30 mg morphine 4 hourly	= 30 mg x 6	= 180 mg over 24 hours = 180 mg MXL od
	OR	= 90 mg MST bd

Once the patient is on controlled-release morphine they should also be prescribed breakthrough doses in case of pain. This is calculated by dividing the total daily dose by six (Example 3).

Example 3

180 mg MXL od   = 180 divided by 6 = 30mg for breakthrough

Exercise 1

Try the following calculations:

1. 40 mg morphine 4 hourly converted to MXL

2. The breakthrough dose of morphine for 200 mg MST bd

3. 60 mg morphine 4 hourly converted to MST

4. The breakthrough dose of morphine for 450 mg MXL

answers on page 64

Read Hanks *et al.* (2001) for more information about the use of opioids in cancer pain. This paper does not, however, specifically address the older person, and there are several differences in their management.

The physiological changes related to ageing have been addressed in previous sections. Ageing does mean that the metabolism of drugs is slower and so the drug may remain at higher doses in the body for longer periods of time. Therefore, clinically, when administering and titrating opiates in the older person, you should use smaller doses and increase doses more slowly. This is one of the reasons why relatively short-acting drugs, such as morphine, are preferable to use for initial titration, rather than long-acting drugs such as fentanyl patches. Not only is it easier to titrate quickly to the correct dose with a short-acting drug, but it is also excreted faster from the body in the case of side effects (Portenoy & Lesage, 1999). Renal and hepatic impairment should be considered and monitored during the period of administration as they can lead to increased drug levels due to reduced excretion.

The side effects of opioids remain the same in the older person as for other groups of patients and include constipation, nausea, sedation, confusion and respiratory depression. Those taking opioids will develop tolerance to all the side effects except constipation and so can be managed as required.

Constipation can be prevented with the prescription of prophylactic aperients at the commencement of opioids, although these are not required with fentanyl as it is less constipating (Becker & Gamlin, 2004). If the patient is stable on short-acting opioids and converted to fentanyl then aperients should be stopped.

Respiratory depression can be created by the action of opioids on the respiratory centre of the brain. However, there is no evidence that elderly cancer patients are at greater risk of this side effect than other groups of patients.

Adjuvant drugs

These can enhance the effect of the opiates or can be used to treat types of pain which are unresponsive to opiates. They include:

corticosteroids – e.g. dexamethasone
Appropriate for pain caused by bone metastases and spinal cord compression. In the older population, their use should be short term due to the increased risk of raised blood sugar and peripheral neuropathy.

tricyclic antidepressants – e.g. Amitriptyline
Used for the treatment of neuropathic pain, which is generally not responsive to conventional analgesia (McGann, 2003). The dose is generally lower than that used for the treatment of depression. The newer antidepressants have not been found to be as effective for pain management. There are many side effects that limit the use of these drugs in the older population (for example, dry mouth, urinary retention and sedation) and they should be discontinued if side effects occur.

anticonvulsants – e.g. gabapentin
Used for the treatment of shooting pain caused by nerve infiltration. Gabapentin is preferable for use in the older population as it has fewer side effects than Carbamazapine and does not require regular blood level monitoring.

bisphosphonates – e.g. pamidronate
Stabilise bone changes caused by lytic bone metastases and have been found to reduce the need for analgesia. When taken orally they tend to have gastro-intestinal side effects and so are usually given intravenously.

cancer treatments – e.g. chemotherapy (including hormone therapy) and radiotherapy
Can be used palliatively to reduce tumour size and associated symptoms. Radiotherapy is especially effective for pain caused by bone metastases.

Answers to exercise 1

1. 240 mg MXL od

2. 65 mg immediate release morphine

3. 180 mg MST bd

4. 75 mg immediate release morphine

Summary

As we have seen, the management of cancer pain in the older population is a complex issue with many aspects to consider. However, unless pain is managed the patient cannot begin to address the many other issues that may be raised by them having cancer. Analgesia may only be one part of the pain management strategy but it is an important part and knowledge of opioids increases confidence in their use and better management for the patient. The physiological changes associated with ageing create additional difficulties, but only increase the need for thorough assessment and individualised management.

References

Becker, R. and Gamlin, R. (2004) *Fundamental Aspects of Palliative Care Nursing*. Wiltshire: Quay Books.

Cherny, N. (2003) Cancer Pain Syndromes. In *Handbook of Pain Management*, ed. R. Melzack and P. Wall. London: Churchill Livingstone.

Cooley, C. and Coventry, G. (2003) Cancer and Older People. *Nursing Older People*, **15**(2), 22–26.

Fukshansky, M., Madhuri, A. and Burton, A. (2005) The Role of Opioids in Cancer Pain Management. *Pain Practice*, **5**(1), 43–54.

Glare, P., Aggarwal, G. and Clark, K. (2004) Ongoing Controversies in the Pharmacological Management of Pain. *Internal Medicine Journal*, **34**, 45–49.

Hanks, G., de Conno, F. and Cherny, N. (2001) Morphine and Alternative Opioids in Cancer Pain: The EAPC recommendations. *British Journal of Cancer*, **85**(5), 587–593.

Maxwell, T. (2000) Cancer Pain Management in the Elderly. *Geriatric Nursing*, **21**(3), 158–163.

McGann, K. (2003) Treating Chronic Pain: The nurse's role and the impact of supplementary prescribing. *Nurse Prescribing*, **1**(3), 120–126.

Mercadante, S., Ferrera, P., Villari, P. and Casuccio, A. (2006) Opioid Escalation in Patients with Cancer Pain: The effect of age. *Journal of Pain and Symptom Management*, **32**(5), 413–419.

Palliative Medicine (2004) Editorial: The World Health Organisation Three-step Analgesic Ladder Comes of Age. *Palliative Medicine*, **18**, 175–176.

Portenoy, R.K. (1992) Pain Management in the Older Cancer Patient. *Oncology*, **6**(2), 86–98.

Portenoy, R.K. and Lesage, P. (1999) Management of Cancer Pain. *The Lancet*, **353**, 1695–1700.

Ward, G. (2000) Pain in Cancer. *Journal of Community Nursing*, **14**(9), 17–18, 20, 22.

Further reading

Saunders, C.M. and Baines, M.J. (1989) *Living With Dying: The management of terminal disease*. Oxford: Oxford University Press.

Schofield, P. and Black, C. (2005) Pain Management in Palliative Care: A case study. *Journal of Community Nursing*, **19**(3), 12–17.

9 Non-pharmacological approaches to pain management in the older person

Catherine Black

As we have seen, pain is a multi-dimensional phenomenon where not all the causes may be physical. It follows that the treatments required to manage the pain may not always be pharmacological (Kearns *et al.*, 2001). In 2002, Turner and Weiner undertook a study to identify what medical students needed to be taught in order to be able to manage chronic pain in older adults. One aspect they identified was to 'understand the role of non-pharmacological modalities in the management of the older adult with chronic pain, for example cognitive behavioural therapy (CBT), physical therapy, exercise, and acupuncture'. They went on to develop the content for a chronic pain curriculum and this included an understanding of the interventions they had identified.

Write a list of the non-pharmacological therapies you are aware of which may be used for pain management.

Underline those that are available in your area.

Identify any that you are not sure how to refer patients for.

There are many different complementary or alternative approaches to medicine (CAM) which can be used in pain management. Menefee and Monti (2005) list 20 different non-pharmacological interventions that are appropriate for use with cancer patients, whilst Wyatt (2002) examines the evidence base for seven different CAM therapies for cancer pain. Both of these papers demonstrate that the use of CAM therapies is being recognised as useful and appropriate within cancer pain management. Whilst this does not necessarily imply that they are also useful and appropriate in chronic pain in the elderly, the categories identified by these authors are useful to demonstrate the range of approaches that can be used.

Category	Example of therapy
Physical interventions	Acupuncture/TENS/application of heat or cold/therapeutic exercise/therapeutic massage/chiropractice/reflexology
Psychological interventions	Cognitive behavioural therapy (CBT)/biofeedback
Mind-body techniques	Relaxation/meditation/hypnosis/imagery/music
Psychosocial interventions	Education/pacing

Middaugh and Pawlick (2002) highlight that multimodal treatments which include both a cognitive behavioural approach and physical interventions are the current best treatment for chronic non-malignant pain. This is supported by the American Geriatric Society (2002) who state that non-pharmacological interventions for chronic pain can work alone or in conjunction with drug regimes.

Middaugh and Pawlick also go on to demonstrate that the older population is often under-represented in such treatment programmes and identify several reasons for this.

The reasons for this discrepancy are unclear, but they acknowledge that they could include:

● health professionals' belief that older patients are less likely to benefit from non-pharmacological or psychological interventions for pain

● health professionals' belief that older patients are less likely to accept non-pharmacological or psychological interventions for pain

● older individuals being less likely to report pain

● older individuals being less likely to seek treatment for their pain.

(Middaugh and Pawlick 2002)

It appears that there are specific reasons why older people are not accessing CAMs for chronic pain and so are under-represented in research on the effectiveness of treatments. This becomes self-perpetuating as while there is little evidence demonstrating the effectiveness of these treatments in this population, the referral rate remains low, and so evidence cannot be established.

|67

This chapter will now focus on areas where there is specific evidence concerning the use of CAM treatment for chronic pain in the older population. This is important as it has been identified that few elderly people rely solely on professional care for management of their chronic pain (Lansbury, 2000) and often use self-care interventions.

PHYSICAL INTERVENTIONS

TRANSCUTANEOUS ELECTRICAL NERVE STIMULATION (TENS)

This is an intervention used for treating chronic pain in all ages. A small electric current from a battery-powered device is passed between two electrodes which are placed on the skin either side of the painful area (Briggs, 2003). The patient can adjust the strength of the current until they get the desired effect. This electrical current is thought to over-excite the a fibres, and so effectively block the c fibres and interfere with any pain messages. It is also associated with endorphin release (Monti & Kunkel, 1998).

Thorsteinsson (1987) undertook a randomised double-blind study with 107 patients with chronic pain using TENS machines and placebo machines. The results showed that there were no problems with using TENS and that, of the 93 patients who finished the study, 43 started to the use TENS at home (46 per cent) and 21 were still using it after six months (23 per cent). He concluded that TENS is indicated in the older population for the following conditions:

- painful peripheral neuropathies
- some postoperative and fracture pain (rib, humerus)
- cancer pain
- back and neck pain
- shoulder pain caused by peri-arthritis.

Gloth and Matesi (2001) highlight that TENS should not be used if the patient has a pacemaker, or on extremities with an IVI in-situ. They also raise the issue that neck stimulation with TENS can increase the risk of vagal effects and so should not be used in the older population.

Thorsteinsson (1987) highlights the point made earlier that TENS is more useful when used alongside other therapies within an overall management plan. He particularly stresses the use of therapeutic exercise in the older population to strengthen the muscles that are causing the pain being controlled by the TENS.

USE OF HEAT AND COLD

Briggs (2003) and Gloth and Matesi (2001) discuss the use of the application of both heat and cold to painful areas as a method of reducing pain.

Cold (cryotherapy) has an analgesic effect by altering nerve transmission, altering blood flow to muscle and nerve, increasing endorphins and reducing muscle spasm. There are several methods of applying cold including ice packs, gel packs, sprays and so on, but there is no evidence that any of these methods are better than others. When treating elderly patients it is important to take precautions for those with impaired sensations and cognition, arterial insufficiency, diseases such as Raynaud's Disease, peripheral neuropathy, cold hypersensitivity and radiotherapy to the area (Briggs, 2003; Gloth & Matesi, 2001).

Heat can be used to promote relaxation, and relieve pain by increasing blood flow, improving tissue healing and 'warming up' joints and muscles for exercise. Locally-applied heating agents such as heat packs can only heat the skin with little effect on underlying tissues. Treatments such as ultrasound can be used for deeper tissues.

As with the use of cryotherapy, heat sensitivity must be established prior to using any treatment. Locally-applied heat should be used cautiously where there is impaired circulation and not at all where there is arterial insufficiency (Gloth & Matesi, 2001).

Contraindications for deep heat include malignancy or bleeding. Precautions should be taken to prevent burns, especially if the patient is sedated or has altered cognition or has impaired local sensation (Briggs, 2003).

Exercise

Relief of musculo-skeletal pain is often short lived if achieved by physical means, such as those noted above, unless accompanied by some exercise to address the underlying musculo-skeletal problem (Gloth & Matesi, 2001; Thorsteinsson, 1987). Studies have shown that in elderly people with chronic musculo-skeletal pain, a regular moderate level exercise programme can reduce their pain and improve their functioning within two to three months.

Appropriate programmes of endurance (walking, swimming), strength (free weights, exercise bands) and circuit training have all been found to be beneficial for the older population. Any associated weight loss is also beneficial for joint pain, and using weights can increase bone density as well as muscle. However, Lansbury's study (2000) did highlight that physiotherapy and exercise were the least preferred strategies for chronic pain management in a group of 72 patients with an age range of 65 to 90 years.

Care must be taken in initial assessment to ensure that the right patients are targeted. Uncontrolled angina, hypertension and diabetes are all contraindications for exercise. The older person's related physical problems may limit their ability to use exercise to help with their pain management (Lansbury, 2000). These can include problems such as fear of falling.

However, Monti and Kunkel (1998) highlight that low level activity can actually increase confidence as well as well-being.

 For more information on physical therapies read Gloth and Matesi (2001).

PSYCHOLOGICAL INTERVENTIONS

COGNITIVE BEHAVIOURAL THERAPY (CBT)

The theory of cognitive interventions in pain management examines issues such as the individual's beliefs and expectations about pain, control of self, abilities to problem solve and existing coping skills (Adams *et al.*, 2006). The use of CBT in chronic pain is based on the 1968 work of Fordyce (cited in Kearns *et al.*, 2001) which suggested that chronic pain could be seen as a behavioural disorder with identifiable behaviours.

Typical pain behaviours may include verbalising pain, grimacing, holding or rubbing body parts, limping, resting, and excessive use of medication. Such behaviours may be displayed in order to receive a response from observers and to maintain a social status and expectations from others associated with having pain. Central to the cognitive behavioural model of pain management is the acceptance that the experience of pain should be, on the whole, private.

The therapy therefore addresses the individual's attitudes, perceptions, beliefs and coping strategies associated with pain through a series of structured appointments where both cognitive and behavioural strategies are used (AGS, 2002). The American Geriatric Society (AGS) (2002) states that CBT usually takes six to ten sessions, of 60 to 90 minutes each.

The sessions may include a variety of interventions, including education, stress management, distraction, cognitive restructuring, problem solving, changing pain behaviours and goal setting (Richardson *et al.*, 2006) amongst others. They focus on helping the patient:

- to address beliefs that their problems are unmanageable

- monitor their emotions, thoughts and behaviours and identify relationships between these and external factors, pain and distress

- learn ways to adapt their thinking and feeling to assist with the development of coping

- use other behaviours such as relaxations, posture (see biofeedback) and exercise (Adams *et al.*, 2006).

Although CBT is the basis for many chronic pain programmes in the UK (Richardson *et al.*, 2006), there is a concern that it may not be an appropriate intervention for elderly people due to a reduction in cognitive ability.

However, the AGS (2002) refutes this and states that the approach is appropriate for all but those with appreciable cognitive impairment, and Middaugh and Pawlick (2002) support the view that age does not affect the effectiveness of such interventions. However, they conclude with the view that although CBT is effective, it does not on its own reduce physical disability in this group of patients (Middaugh & Pawlick, 2002).

BIOFEEDBACK

Biofeedback is a technique that involves the patient being taught how to recognise automatic body behaviours and responses (for example, heart rate or muscle tension) and so learn to control involuntary responses consciously. It is often combined with CBT. Monitors can be used to visualise the changes but the technique can be taught without them.

Middaugh and Pawlick (2002) discuss a number of studies where biofeedback has been used to successfully manage chronic pain in the older population. They identify that several changes need to be made to the sessions in order for this group of patients to benefit fully. These changes include:

- modifying the standard treatment programmes to ensure that patients can hear and understand the instructions, with the therapist talking more slowly and clearly
- checking comprehension after instruction
- summarising and repeating instructions in the following sessions
- increasing the session length so as not to be rushed.

Such changes have ensured that the success rate for using biofeedback to manage chronic headaches, for example, is the same (50 to 70 per cent) for older and younger patients.

MIND-BODY TECHNIQUES

RELAXATION

Relaxation is often combined with CBT and biofeedback to increase the multimodal efficacy of interventions. One of its benefits is that of increasing an overall sense of well-being (Richardson *et al.*, 2006). Patients can be encouraged to achieve muscle relaxation by contracting and relaxing muscle in a systematic way.

The use of biofeedback to identify other body changes can enhance the approach, although such a combination increases the difficulty of research identifying which intervention is effective. However, Middaugh and Pawlick (2002) do identify that the evidence supports the fact that older people respond as effectively to biofeedback-assisted relaxation as younger people and show similar responses physiologically. Key nursing skills are used to support and aid relaxation including assessment, communication and evaluation (Richardson *et al.*, 2006)

MUSIC

McCaffrey and Freeman (2003) undertook a randomised controlled study with 66 elderly patients with chronic osteoarthritis pain. They used the SF-MPQ to assess pain in the two groups over 14 days. The experimental group were required to sit in a comfortable chair, with no distractions, for one hour a day listening to a tape of relaxing classical music. The control group were required to sit in a comfortable chair, with no distractions, for the same period.

Pain was assessed after the hour on days 1, 7 and 14. The experimental group showed statistically and clinically less pain than the control group on all three days with the experimental group showing a reduction in their pain scores whilst pain scores remained the same for the control group.

71

Whilst this is only related to pain caused by one problem, it does show that music can be a useful intervention to utilise. Listening to music is a cost-effective intervention which can be easily incorporated into patient care and is beneficial for elderly people with pain.

PSYCHOSOCIAL INTERVENTIONS

EDUCATION

Education is an important part of all healthcare practice. Information can decrease stress and increase coping, and also improve adherence to treatment regimes. All of the interventions discussed in this chapter require a degree of patient education. It must be at an appropriate level and pace for the individual. It can also be supported by written information to assist the patient to manage the situation at home. Self-help and support groups can be a source of information and advice as well as peer support and the practitioner should identify those that are in their area.

PACING

This refers to helping the patients to structure their activities so that they don't increase their tiredness and so negatively impact on their level of function and pain. They need to try and ensure that they do not cycle between over- and under-activity but instead maintain steady levels. The baseline for activity should be reasonable and achievable and the patient may need support in identifying this.

Summary

This chapter has highlighted some of the non-pharmacological approaches to pain management currently available and especially those where there is supportive research for their use in the older population with chronic pain. In order to utilise such approaches effectively, you need to be aware where such services are in your area and how to refer to them. Only in this way can you ensure that you utilise all the resources available and take a truly multimodal approach to pain management within your practice.

References

Adams, N., Poole, H. and Richardson, C. (2006) Psychological Approaches to Chronic Pain Management: Part 1. *Journal of Clinical Nursing*, **15**, 290–300.

American Geriatrics Society (AGS) (2002) The Management of Persistent Pain in Older Persons. *Journal of the American Geriatrics Society*, **50**(6) (Suppl.), S205–S224.

Briggs, E. (2003) The Nursing Management of Pain in Older People. *Nursing Standard*, **17**(18), 47–55.

Gloth, M. and Matesi, A. (2001) Physical Therapy and Exercise in Pain Management. *Clinics in Geriatric Medicine*, **17**(3), 525–535.

Kearns, R.D., Otis, J.D. and Stein Marcus, K. (2001) Cognitive-behavioural Therapy for Chronic Pain in the Elderly. *Clinics in Geriatric Medicine*, **17**(3), 503–523. Lansbury, G. (2000) Chronic Pain Management: A qualitative study of elderly people's preferred coping strategies and barriers to management. *Journal of Disability and Rehabilitation*, **22**(1–2), 2–14.

McCaffrey, R. and Freeman, E. (2003) Effect of Music on Chronic Osteoarthritis Pain in Older People. *Journal of Advanced Nursing*, **44**(5), 517–524.

Menefee, L. and Monti, D. (2005) Nonpharmacological and Complementary Approaches to Cancer Pain Management. *Journal of American Osteopathic Association*, **105**(11) (Suppl. 5), S15–S20.

Middaugh, S.J. and Pawlick, K. (2002) Biofeedback and Behavioural Treatment of a Persistent Pain in the Older Adult: A review and a study. *Applied Psychophysiology and Biofeedback*, **27**(3), 185–202.

Monti, D. and Kunkel, E. (1998) Management of Chronic Pain among Elderly Patients. *Psychiatric Services*, **49**(12), 1537–1539.

Richardson, C., Adams, N. and Poole, H. (2006) Psychological Approaches for the Nursing Management of Chronic Pain: Part 2. *Journal of Clinical Nursing*, **15**, 1196–1202

Thorsteinsson, G. (1987) Chronic Pain: Use of TENS in the elderly. *Geriatrics*, **42**(12), 75–82.

Wyatt, G. (2002) Complementary Therapies: Emerging strategies for pain management. *Cancer Practice*, **10**(Suppl. 1), S70–S73.

Appendix 1: Case studies

Within this workbook we have attempted to help you to consider your own practice while learning about the principles of pain management. The following case studies are intended to help you to consolidate this learning. All are based on the theories that we have explored so, if you can't remember, just refer back. Answers are at the end of this section.

CASE STUDY 1

An 85-year-old woman is seated in her living room recliner when you arrive. Her medical history includes insulin-dependent diabetes and a longstanding problem with osteoporosis. Two months ago she was diagnosed with several vertebral compression fractures of her lumbar spine. The reason for your visit is a weekly check of her blood pressure, blood glucose and healing decubitus ulcer on her heel. Her husband tells you she has not been able to lie down and sleep in her bed for days. She has been able to 'cat nap' but only if exhausted from lack of sleep. Her uneaten breakfast sits next to her and, when questioned, she says that she is in too much pain to eat or drink. She is unable to give her pain a numeric rating saying 'it hurts like always' and 'it's been worse than this before'.

Her 83-year old husband shows you her drawer of medications. Many of the medication bottles are still full and the pain medications have been prescribed by several different doctors from the practice as well as from the hospital.

- MS Contin – 15 mg 12 hrly
- Oramorph syrup – 10 mg 2–4 hrly PRN (as needed)
- Co-Proxamol – 2 tablets 6 hrly PRN, alternate with:
  - Paracetamol – 1 gm PRN
  - Diclofenac – 50 mg OD
  - Amitriptylline – 25 mg nocte
  - Temazepam – 15 mg nocte

On further assessment, her husband informs you she has been taking the morphine sulphate during the day (3–4 times). She has been saving the MS-Contin for when the pain is really bad, meaning that she usually takes it once a week.

The primary goals of this case are to consider:

- the risks of multiple drug therapy (polypharmacy) such as:
  - confusion about dosing regime
  - difficulty in determining which drug is causing a particular side effect
- alternative pain assessment tools
- the holistic approach to pain assessment.

1. What other pain assessment tools could be used instead of the Numerical Rating Scale?

2. What other factors do we need to consider in the pain assessment?

3. What problems do you see with her analgesic orders?

4. How could we simplify her analgesic regime?

5. What analgesic orders would you recommend to her physician?

CASE STUDY 2

You make a routine post-operative visit to the home of a 65-year-old man with COPD who underwent knee arthroscopy yesterday. According to his wife he has slept 'off and on' since he arrived home. On assessment, this patient reports knee pain on a scale of 7 out of 10. He says that the 'pain pills' make him dizzy and nauseous but that they do take the edge off the pain for 1–2 hours. He has taken Tylex tablets about every 4–5 hours since arriving home yesterday. He tells you that the nurse on the ward had told him not to take anything stronger because of his COPD.

1. What additional information do you need to communicate the patient's analgesic needs to the physician?

2. How would you report John's pain assessment to his physician?

3. What is the risk of respiratory depression if we increase the dose of opioid? What are the risk factors?

4. What alternative analgesic regime would you suggest?

   a. Tylex X 2

   b. Ibuprofen 400 mg 6 hrly

   c. Morphine 15 mg 4 hrly

CASE STUDY 3

Mrs Jones is an 85-year-old resident of a care home that you visit. She complains of troublesome burning pain in both feet which keeps her awake at night. The primary care physician has diagnosed painful diabetic neuropathy and prescribed Paracetamol at night. This worked for a while but the pain has now returned. Mrs Jones has a history of diabetes, hypertension and occasional falls.

1. What other analgesic drugs may be appropriate for this pain?

2. What drugs are used to treat neuropathic pain?

3. What are the classic barriers to pain management that are often perceived by older adults?

4. What complementary approaches may be used to deal with this pain?

CASE STUDY 4

Mrs Green is an 89-year-old lady who lives in a care home. She suffers from Alzheimer's Disease, osteoarthritis, deafness and visual impairment. Up until recently, she was able to walk with the aid of a zimmer frame and two nurses. Now she is unable to move without obvious signs of distress and when she sits out of bed she cries out in pain, rubbing her knees and making unusual grunting noises.

1. Can you list some of the classic pain behaviours reported in the literature?

2. What are the classic barriers to pain management held by staff?

3. What pain assessment tools could we use to measure her pain?

4. What would be an appropriate analgesic regime?

Answers to case study 1

1. ● Visual Analogue Scale or Colour Scale

   ● Faces Pain Scale (should be avoided with older adults)

   ● Verbal Descriptors (none, mild, moderate, severe)

   ● Journal of activity or other behaviour clues that may be provided by her husband.

2. Remember that we have previously identified that pain assessment is not merely about intensity alone. It is much more complex than that and needs to address quality, location, factors influencing and so on.

3. ● Multiple opioids, inappropriate dosing intervals, unclear hierarchy, too many prescribers.

   ● The instructions on some are unclear – for example 'take as needed' or 'alternate with'.

   ● NSAIDs have the potential for renal toxicity.

   ● The Amitriptylline dose is too low and Amitriptylline is contraindicated in older adults. However, Amitriptylline is sometimes used to treat insomnia in older adults – it could have been prescribed for that purpose.

   ● The dose of anti-depressants should be gradually increased to effect.

   ● There is a possibility of Paracetamol toxicity.

4. ● Use morphine only and one NSAID.

   ● Provide a written pain management plan and possibly a journal or log that tells the patient and her husband when to take the scheduled medicines and how to record the PRN doses.

Answers to case study 2

1. ● What is the impact of the pain? Is he eating and what does sleeping 'off and on' really mean?

   ● Is the patient experiencing problems with sedation? Are there any other side effects?

   ● What was his previous response to analgesics like codeine, oxycodone, NSAIDs? Would the addition of an NSAID give additional benefit?

   ● Does John have a bowel management programme?

   ● What is a reasonable pain goal for John?

2. You need to record the intensity, along with the quality of the pain, and be certain that the location is the same as his previous surgery.

3. Clinically significant respiratory depression is rare, particularly if the dose and strength of the medicine matches the severity of the pain. Risk factors for respiratory depression include:

   ● rapid dose escalation, especially if the patient is opioid naïve

   ● older age

   ● concomitant use of other CNS depressants such as benzodiazepines, alcohol and older antihistamines

   ● over-rapid increase in dose of drugs with long half lives.

4. There is not just one correct answer here. You need to be cautious about excess Tylex consumption and give tips about managing nausea and sedation and preventing constipation.

Answers to case study 3

1. Neuropathic pain tends to be less sensitive to simple analgesic drugs. Although a trial of Paracetamol may be appropriate for a while, if this does not work it may be appropriate to use a combination analgesia regime such as Paracetamol and Codeine. Tramadol may be another alternative.

2. Initially, a prescription of Amitriptylline 10 mg at night may help the pain and the sleep. The dose could then be increased every third day to 30mg. Alternatively Gabapentin 100 mg at night may be introduced. Paracetamol could be continued at a dose of 1 gm 6 hrly.

3. • A fear of addiction.

   • A lack of understanding that pain management is their right.

   • A fear of side effects.

   • A belief that pain is inevitable.

4. Use of tricyclic antidepressants may reduce the pain to a more tolerable level but it is unlikely to eradicate the pain totally. Therefore, it may be appropriate to introduce other strategies to aid sleep. For example, relaxation, distraction or creating a more positive sleep environment.

Answers to case study 4

1. • Facial expression

   • Fidgeting/restlessness

   • Changed behaviour

   • Aggression/abusiveness

   • Crying/whimpering

   • Tension/guarding/protection

   • Observations (raised blood pressure, pulse and respirations may indicate pain)

2. • A belief that older adults cannot tolerate opioids.

   • A persistent use of traditional methods.

   • A belief that the failure to express pain indicates an absence of pain.

   • A perception that pain decreases with age.

3. • Abbey or Doloplus Pain Scales

   • NOPAIN (more appropriate for care assistants to use)

4. A low dose of oral morphine (5 mg) would be useful to assist with mobility. This could be titrated and translated to slow-release morphine later. Constipation would need to be anticipated and also nausea. A physiotherapy referral would enable gradual mobility improvements.

Appendix 2: Test your knowledge

PAIN QUIZ

1. What is the incidence of pain in the community and in care homes?

2. What is the World Health Organisation classification of 'elderly'?

3. What common pain syndromes are seen in older adults?

4. What is the name given to pain receptors?

5. Which nociceptors respond to vibration?

6. Pain is felt as a result of which type of stimulation?

7. Where are opioid receptors located?

8. Where is the pain gate located?

9. What is the role of the thalamus in pain processing?

10. What is the role of the limbic system in pain processing?

11. What is the role of the reticular activating system in pain processing?

12. What is the pain threshold?

13. What factors influence the pain threshold?

14. What are the external factors that influence the pain threshold?

15. What are the common types of dementia?

Answers can be found throughout this book.

KEY WORD DEFINITIONS

Fill in the meanings for these key words.

A-delta _____

A-beta _____

Nociceptive pain _____

Neuropathic pain _____

Myelin sheath _____

Prostaglandins _____

Dorsal horn _____

Spinothalamic tract _____

Substantia gelatinosa _____

Chronic pain _____

Dementia _____

Adjuvant _____

Kinesthetic _____

Ageism _____

Opiophobia _____

CAM _____

TENS _____

WORD SEARCH

Now have a go at this!

M	D	O	L	O	P	L	U	S	S	S	L	R	N	A	E	O	S	I	I	E	E	C	T
E	L	C	I	M	H	E	E	N	G	E	N	D	E	R	U	T	H	A	L	A	M	U	S
T	E	A	R	N	Y	N	I	E	N	I	N	O	T	O	R	E	S	A	S	I	G	Y	A
S	S	R	O	M	S	H	C	G	A	R	N	D	E	N	E	Y	C	E	O	E	D	L	R
Y	E	E	U	E	I	I	I	P	O	O	N	M	O	Z	O	S	T	A	K	Y	M	U	P
S	N	N	N	T	O	E	P	S	N	C	F	I	B	R	E	S	V	N	A	T	L	N	O
G	R	I	Y	S	L	G	S	E	T	P	T	L	I	U	P	L	P	R	L	O	T	I	S
N	O	H	N	Y	O	U	U	C	A	A	L	G	G	N	H	E	S	O	C	A	A	S
I	E	P	S	S	G	R	C	N	X	I	M	O	E	I	V	D	I	N	U	N	D	P	N
I	I	R	E	C	Y	O	Y	A	I	E	L	I	M	H	D	A	A	N	S	I	E	E	C
A	S	O	N	I	T	A	L	E	G	A	I	T	N	A	T	S	B	U	S	A	L	T	V
V	M	M	K	B	N	E	E	O	N	F	P	E	L	E	T	E	A	T	S	P	T	U	L
I	G	E	E	M	R	N	C	A	I	V	P	C	B	N	A	E	R	N	A	R	A	C	S
T	M	T	P	I	H	P	L	I	U	M	I	A	I	E	L	A	C	S	S	E	C	A	F
C	G	R	H	L	C	A	D	C	A	S	E	R	U	H	C	M	A	A	I	C	T	D	R
A	D	O	A	R	U	A	M	S	E	R	E	D	O	T	T	T	M	I	R	N	S	S	E
R	E	K	L	S	P	N	S	G	E	O	U	H	I	N	O	A	E	D	U	A	A	O	S
A	S	N	I	D	N	A	L	G	A	T	S	O	R	P	M	O	P	S	P	C	P	I	T
L	N	V	N	N	G	A	R	I	M	P	N	U	A	N	E	E	A	O	I	L	S	E	L
U	V	B	S	E	N	E	N	I	B	E	N	I	A	P	C	I	N	O	R	H	C	A	E
C	A	U	L	A	C	U	P	U	N	C	T	U	R	E	H	M	N	T	E	U	T	O	P
I	A	A	A	D	R	A	T	T	O	I	A	I	C	I	T	D	O	I	U	G	E	O	P
T	C	A	L	S	R	C	Y	E	N	C	O	M	M	U	N	I	C	A	T	I	O	N	I
E	L	A	C	S	Y	E	B	B	A	O	E	I	R	A	N	L	N	P	I	A	A	S	U
R	M	E	A	L	U	A	O	U	A	N	O	A	L	F	H	S	V	G	S	M	H	I	B

Find the hidden words listed below by tracking in straight lines horizontally, vertically or diagonally, in any direction.

PHYSIOLOGY
ANALGESIC LADDER
A DELTA
RELAXATION
C FIBRES
DISTRACTION
RETICULAR ACTIVATING SYSTEM
VISUAL ANALOGUE SCALE

LIMBIC SYSTEM
FACES SCALE
A BETA
ABBEY SCALE
NOCICEPTORS
DOLOPLUS
NEUROPATHIC PAIN
ACUPUNCTURE
GENDER
MASSAGE

CULTURE
NSAIDS
THALAMUS
COMMUNICATION
SUBSTANTIA GELATINOSA
SNOEZELEN
ACUTE PAIN
SENSORY ENVIRONMENT

CHRONIC PAIN
CANCER PAIN
ENDORPHINS
PROSTAGLANDINS
ENKEPHALINS
SEROTONIN
MORPHINE
HISTAMINE
PARACETAMOL
EPIDEMIOLOGY

Appendix 3: Further reading and resources

To complete your understanding of the issues in pain management for older people you may wish to access some of the following materials.

Textbooks

Broome, A. (1987) *Living with Pain*. London: British Psychological Society.

Carroll, D. and Bowsher, D. (1994) *Pain Management and Nursing Care*. Oxford: Butterworth Heinemann.

Carr, E. and Mann, E. (2000) *Pain: Creative approaches to effective management*. Basingstoke: Macmillan Press.

Carter, B. (1998) *Perspectives on Pain: Mapping the territory*. London: Arnold.

Davis, B. (2000) *Caring for People in Pain*. London: Routledge.

Hawthorne, J. and Redmond, K. (1998) *Pain: Causes and management*. London: Blackwell Science.

McCaffery, M. and Beebe, A. (1994) *Clinical Manual for Nursing Practice*. London: C.V. Mosby.

Melzack, R. and Wall, P. (1992) *The Challenge of Pain*. London: Penguin Books.

Turk, D. and Melzack, R. (1992) *Handbook of Pain Assessment*. Guildford: Guildford Press.

Schofield, P.A. (2007) *The Management of Pain in Older People*. Chichester: Wiley.

Journal articles

Davis, G.C., Heimenz, M.L. and White, T.L. (2002) Barriers to Managing Chronic Pain of Older Adults with Arthritis. *Journal of Nursing Scholarship*, **34**(2), 121–126.

Local policies and procedures

National Service Frameworks – Older People (2000) Department of Health HMSO

International Association for the Study of Pain (IASP) – www.iasp.org

The British Pain Society – www.britishpainsociety.org

You may also like to seek help and support from staff familiar with the care of this group of patients.